M000220259

TO READ OR ~~NOT~~ TO READ

A LITERARY JOURNAL FOR THE BOOK LOVER'S SOUL

This journal belongs to

TO READ OR ~~NOT~~ TO READ

ISBN 978-0-525-65433-9

Published in the United States by WaterBrook, an imprint of Random House, a division of Penguin Random House LLC, New York.

INK & WILLOW and its colophon are trademarks of Penguin Random House LLC.

Printed in China

Cover and interior design by Laura Palese

10 9 8 7 6 5 4 3 2 1

2020—First Edition

SPECIAL SALES

Once you learn to read, you will be forever free.

—Frederick Douglass

As all book lovers know, few things in life are as enjoyable as getting lost in a good book. Even more thrilling is the prospect of new books to discover and enjoy. Thus, we have created *To Read or ~~Not~~ to Read: A Literary Journal for the Book Lover's Soul* so you can log and review your current reads as well as discover new books and authors to add to your TBR pile. In addition, there are many other fun features, including quizzes, space to jot down quotes, a list of book-related holidays, and more. Other special features include:

MY TOP PICKS—*record your favorite authors, characters, literary crushes, and more*

AUTHOR SPOTLIGHTS—*learn about six lesser-known authors who have influenced the Christian faith*

LITERARY MATCHUPS—*select your personal preferences from several fun lists*

A DIY TABLE OF CONTENTS—*write in the books you review for easy reference*

No matter your preferred genre, you'll find countless suggestions for your reading pleasure. We hope this journal becomes a treasured keepsake that allows you to remember the books that have influenced you.

CONTENTS

Write in the titles of the books you review for easy reference.

DATE PUBLISHED

DATE READ

MY RATING

WHY I READ THIS BOOK

IT INSPIRED ME TO (READ/LEARN/VISIT)

I WILL RECOMMEND IT TO

BOOK TITLE

AUTHOR

FICTION GENRE

NONFICTION TOPIC

NOTES

MY REVIEW

FINAL TAKEAWAY

Fill your house with stacks of books,
in all the crannies and all the nooks.

—Dr. Seuss

DATE PUBLISHED

DATE READ

MY RATING

WHY I READ THIS BOOK

IT INSPIRED ME TO (READ/LEARN/VISIT)

I WILL RECOMMEND IT TO

BOOK TITLE

AUTHOR

FICTION GENRE

NONFICTION TOPIC

NOTES

MY REVIEW

FINAL TAKEAWAY

The original name Charles Dickens used for Tiny Tim was "Little Fred."

DATE PUBLISHED

DATE READ

MY RATING

WHY I READ THIS BOOK

IT INSPIRED ME TO (READ/LEARN/VISIT)

I WILL RECOMMEND IT TO

BOOK TITLE

AUTHOR

☐ FICTION GENRE

☐ NONFICTION TOPIC

NOTES

MY REVIEW

FINAL TAKEAWAY

Once you have read a book you care about,
some part of it is always with you.

—LOUIS L'AMOUR

✧ DATE PUBLISHED ✧

✧ DATE READ ✧

✧ MY RATING ✧

WHY I READ THIS BOOK

IT INSPIRED ME TO (READ/LEARN/VISIT)

I WILL RECOMMEND IT TO

BOOK TITLE

AUTHOR

☐ FICTION GENRE

☐ NONFICTION TOPIC

NOTES

MY REVIEW ______

FINAL TAKEAWAY ______

The word for loving the smell of old books is bibliosmia.

◇ DATE PUBLISHED ◇

◇ DATE READ ◇

◇ MY RATING ◇

WHY I READ THIS BOOK

IT INSPIRED ME TO (READ/LEARN/VISIT)

I WILL RECOMMEND IT TO

BOOK TITLE

AUTHOR

☐ FICTION GENRE

☐ NONFICTION TOPIC

NOTES

MY REVIEW

FINAL TAKEAWAY

If you only read the books that everyone else is reading, you can only think what everyone else is thinking.

—Haruki Murakami

✧ DATE PUBLISHED ✧

✧ DATE READ ✧

✧ MY RATING ✧

WHY I READ THIS BOOK

IT INSPIRED ME TO (READ/LEARN/VISIT)

I WILL RECOMMEND IT TO

BOOK TITLE

AUTHOR

☐ FICTION GENRE

☐ NONFICTION TOPIC

NOTES

MY REVIEW

FINAL TAKEAWAY

The Dead Sea Scrolls, discovered in 1947 by a Bedouin boy searching for a lost goat, are the oldest copies of Jewish text in existence.

DATE PUBLISHED

DATE READ

MY RATING

WHY I READ THIS BOOK

IT INSPIRED ME TO (READ/LEARN/VISIT)

I WILL RECOMMEND IT TO

BOOK TITLE

AUTHOR

☐ FICTION GENRE

☐ NONFICTION TOPIC

NOTES

MY REVIEW

FINAL TAKEAWAY

She read books as one would breathe air,
to fill up and live.

—Annie Dillard

✧ DATE PUBLISHED ✧

✧ DATE READ ✧

✧ MY RATING ✧

WHY I READ THIS BOOK

IT INSPIRED ME TO (READ/LEARN/VISIT)

I WILL RECOMMEND IT TO

BOOK TITLE

AUTHOR

☐ FICTION GENRE

☐ NONFICTION TOPIC

NOTES

MY REVIEW

FINAL TAKEAWAY

Paperback books were introduced by Penguin in the 1930s, revolutionizing books as something other than a luxury item.

DATE PUBLISHED

DATE READ

MY RATING

WHY I READ THIS BOOK

IT INSPIRED ME TO (READ/LEARN/VISIT)

I WILL RECOMMEND IT TO

BOOK TITLE

AUTHOR

☐ FICTION GENRE

☐ NONFICTION TOPIC

NOTES

MY REVIEW

FINAL TAKEAWAY

A room without books is like a body without a soul.

—Marcus Tullius Cicero

✧ DATE PUBLISHED ✧

✧ DATE READ ✧

✧ MY RATING ✧

WHY I READ THIS BOOK

IT INSPIRED ME TO (READ/LEARN/VISIT)

I WILL RECOMMEND IT TO

BOOK TITLE

AUTHOR

☐ FICTION GENRE

☐ NONFICTION TOPIC

NOTES

MY REVIEW

FINAL TAKEAWAY

The phrase "a sight for sore eyes" originated in 1738 in A Complete Collection of Genteel and Ingenious Conversation *by Jonathan Swift, author of* Gulliver's Travels.

✧ DATE PUBLISHED ✧

✧ DATE READ ✧

✧ MY RATING ✧

WHY I READ THIS BOOK

IT INSPIRED ME TO (READ/LEARN/VISIT)

I WILL RECOMMEND IT TO

BOOK TITLE

AUTHOR

☐ FICTION

☐ NONFICTION

GENRE

TOPIC

NOTES

MY REVIEW

FINAL TAKEAWAY

Keep reading. It's one of the most marvelous adventures anyone can have.

—Lloyd Alexander

DATE PUBLISHED

DATE READ

MY RATING

WHY I READ THIS BOOK

IT INSPIRED ME TO (READ/LEARN/VISIT)

I WILL RECOMMEND IT TO

BOOK TITLE

AUTHOR

☐ FICTION GENRE

☐ NONFICTION TOPIC

NOTES

MY REVIEW

FINAL TAKEAWAY

Antoine de Saint-Exupéry's 1943 book The Little Prince *has been read by more than 400 million children and adults worldwide and is still considered a bestseller today.*

DATE PUBLISHED

DATE READ

MY RATING

WHY I READ THIS BOOK

IT INSPIRED ME TO (READ/LEARN/VISIT)

I WILL RECOMMEND IT TO

BOOK TITLE

AUTHOR

- [ ] FICTION — GENRE
- [ ] NONFICTION — TOPIC

NOTES

MY REVIEW

FINAL TAKEAWAY

A book is a dream that you hold in your hand.

—Neil Gaiman

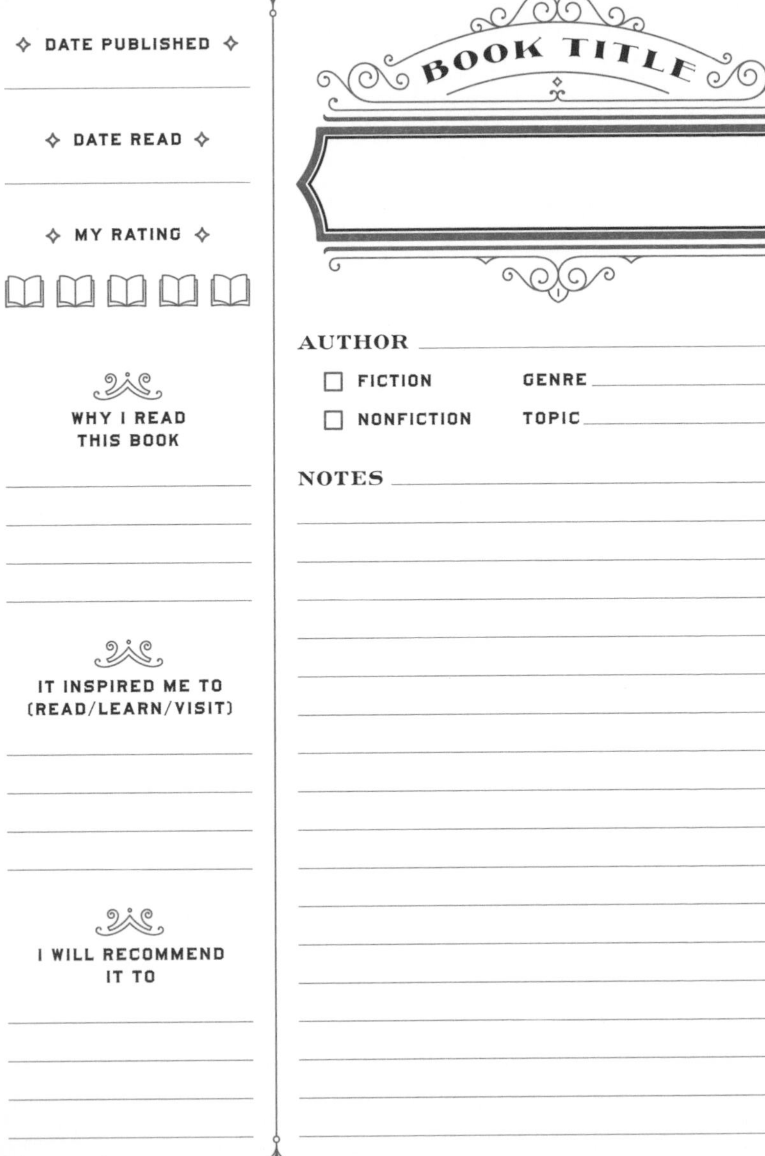

DATE PUBLISHED
DATE READ
MY RATING
WHY I READ THIS BOOK
IT INSPIRED ME TO (READ/LEARN/VISIT)
I WILL RECOMMEND IT TO
BOOK TITLE
AUTHOR
FICTION
NONFICTION
GENRE
TOPIC
NOTES

MY REVIEW

FINAL TAKEAWAY

In 1810, the Scoville Memorial Library in Salisbury, Connecticut, opened as the first publicly funded library in the United States and the first to offer its services free of charge.

DATE PUBLISHED

DATE READ

MY RATING

WHY I READ THIS BOOK

IT INSPIRED ME TO (READ/LEARN/VISIT)

I WILL RECOMMEND IT TO

BOOK TITLE

AUTHOR

☐ FICTION GENRE

☐ NONFICTION TOPIC

NOTES

MY REVIEW

FINAL TAKEAWAY

The story is truly finished—and meaning is made—not when the author adds the last period, but when the reader enters.

—Celeste Ng

FLANNERY O'CONNOR

BIRTH	GENRE	AWARDS
March 25, 1925 *Savannah, Georgia* DEATH *August 3, 1964* *Milledgeville, Georgia*	*American fiction* POPULAR WORKS A Good Man Is Hard to Find (and Other Stories), Wise Blood, The Violent Bear It Away	*National Book Award for fiction*

"PLEASE HELP me dear God to be a good writer and to get something else accepted" was the simple prayer penned by a young University of Iowa student during the mid-1940s. With the subsequent publication of two novels, more than thirty short stories, and dozens of essays and reviews, the prayer of Flannery O'Connor was answered. She is now widely considered to be one of the most gifted writers in the sphere of American literature.

A devout believer all her life, O'Connor was intentional in making sure her art always pointed to God. "Don't let me ever think, dear God," she wrote, "that I was anything but the instrument for Your story." Even though violence, suffering, and darkness of the soul often appeared in her work, a closer analysis of her writing reveals her determination to depict the world and humanity as they are—fallen and in desperate need of grace. Drawing from the belief that God can be found even in the darkest circumstances, O'Connor took it upon herself to seek out joy wherever it was least expected. "Please help me to get down under things and find where You are," she prayed.

"Stalking joy" became a daily reality for the young writer when at the age of twenty-five she began what would become a fourteen-year struggle with lupus. Though the disease tragically cut her life short at thirty-nine, her conviction to her faith both in her writing and her personal life stands as a testament to the message that grace triumphs over suffering.

HOW BOOKISH ARE YOU?

Mark the statements below that describe your relationship with books. Then calculate your score to discover how bookish you really are.

- ☐ You often stay up late to finish a book—eating and sleeping are just inconveniences to what *really* matters!
- ☐ Sometimes you're late to appointments because you need to finish a chapter.
- ☐ You watch every movie adaptation of your favorite books—and *of course* the book was better.
- ☐ Your favorite pastime is browsing the shelves at your local bookstore.
- ☐ You complete the book you're reading even if you're not loving it. Gotta meet that Goodreads goal!
- ☐ You always have a book with you so you can read whenever there's a free moment.
- ☐ Your weekend plans always include curling up with a good book.
- ☐ You don't have a to-be-read pile—you have *piles*...upon piles upon piles.
- ☐ During your nine-to-five, you often think about diving back into your current read *right* when you get home.
- ☐ You spend hours organizing your bookshelf by color, author, or genre.
- ☐ You own book-themed clothes, mugs, prints, and/or stickers.
- ☐ You're truly sad when you finish a book. It's *literally* like closing a chapter on part of your life.
- ☐ You read or listen to an audiobook during your commute to work.
- ☐ One of your New Year's resolutions is the number of books you plan to read.
- ☐ You often begin conversations by asking, "What are you reading?"
- ☐ Your friends consider you the go-to person for book recommendations—they know they can always trust you to introduce them to their next favorite read.
- ☐ You pack multiple books in your suitcase when traveling, even if you know you won't get to all of them.
- ☐ You buy additional copies of your favorite book to make sure your friends and family members also fall in love with it.
- ☐ Every payday, you calculate how many books you can buy after rent, utilities, food, and all of the other "essentials."
- ☐ You equate free time with reading time. What else would you possibly be doing?
- ☐ Your birthday and Christmas wish lists are made up almost entirely of books.

- ☐ You consider naming your children or pets after your favorite authors and/or characters, if you haven't already.
- ☐ When you decide to socialize, you suggest hanging out in a bookstore, getting together for a book club, or going to a local author event.
- ☐ You text your friends when your favorite author likes your Instagram post.
- ☐ You don't mind when someone is running late for a get-together. Extra reading time!
- ☐ After finishing a book, you often jump online to see what other readers thought of the ending—and if they didn't like it as much as you, they're obviously wrong!
- ☐ You immediately get excited when you wake up and realize you still have several chapters left in your current read.
- ☐ You find yourself talking about characters as if they're your real friends—and when people ask who that is, you sigh in disappointment before explaining.
- ☐ After finishing a book, you immediately update your progress on Goodreads so you're closer to completing your annual reading challenge.
- ☐ You regularly experience mild levels of *abibliophobia*, the fear of running out of reading material.
- ☐ You've been known to set Google alerts or obsessively follow your favorite author's social posts when you're waiting for the next book in the series. After all, what could they possibly be doing that's more important than finishing their next book!

SCORING

1-11 REASONABLY BOOKISH

You may love reading, but it hasn't taken over your life—yet. You're not afraid to admit that you love a good book or to make recommendations to your friends. However, you also value your sleep and your human friendships, so you make sure those are higher up on your list of priorities.

12-21 UNDOUBTEDLY BOOKISH

No one would mistake you for a non-reader. You spend your free time at your local library or with your book club, and there's no hiding the stacks of books in your home when guests come over. But you're proud to be a book nerd and love sharing in the joy of reading with others.

22-31 TIME-FOR-AN-INTERVENTION BOOKISH

You live and breathe books. You wouldn't be caught dead without a good read in your backpack or purse, and you dream of a life that allows you to read all day, every day. When your friends call to make sure you're alive, you have to assure them you're just consumed by your latest read.

MY TOP PICKS

MY FAVORITE AUTHOR

PLACES IN BOOKS I MOST WANT TO VISIT

CHARACTERS' HOMES I MOST WANT TO OWN

CHARACTERS MOST LIKE ME

CHARACTERS I'D MOST WANT TO BE

CHARACTERS I'D MOST WANT AS FRIENDS

BEST LITERARY HEROES

BEST LITERARY VILLAINS

BOOKS I LEARNED THE MOST FROM

MOST ROMANTIC LITERARY COUPLES

BOOKS THAT IMPACTED MY FAITH THE MOST

MY LITERARY CRUSHES

MOST QUOTABLE AUTHOR / CHARACTER

AUTHOR I'VE READ THE MOST

FUNNIEST CHARACTER

AUTHORS I MOST WANT TO MEET

DATE PUBLISHED

DATE READ

MY RATING

WHY I READ THIS BOOK

IT INSPIRED ME TO (READ/LEARN/VISIT)

I WILL RECOMMEND IT TO

BOOK TITLE

AUTHOR

- [ ] FICTION GENRE
- [ ] NONFICTION TOPIC

NOTES

MY REVIEW

FINAL TAKEAWAY

The King James Bible is the most widely distributed book in history, with more than 6 billion copies in print.

DATE PUBLISHED

DATE READ

MY RATING

WHY I READ THIS BOOK

IT INSPIRED ME TO (READ/LEARN/VISIT)

I WILL RECOMMEND IT TO

BOOK TITLE

AUTHOR

☐ FICTION GENRE

☐ NONFICTION TOPIC

NOTES

MY REVIEW

FINAL TAKEAWAY

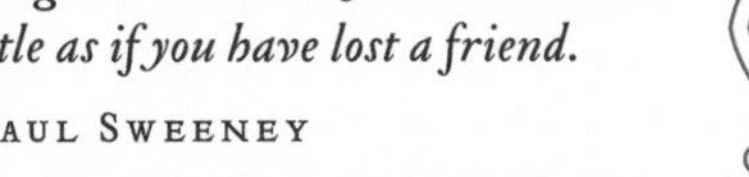

You know you've read a good book when you turn the last page and feel a little as if you have lost a friend.

—Paul Sweeney

DATE PUBLISHED

DATE READ

MY RATING

WHY I READ THIS BOOK

IT INSPIRED ME TO (READ/LEARN/VISIT)

I WILL RECOMMEND IT TO

BOOK TITLE

AUTHOR

FICTION GENRE

NONFICTION TOPIC

NOTES

MY REVIEW

FINAL TAKEAWAY

A Dictionary of the English Language was published in 1755, the product of an initiative of publishers and booksellers in London who desired standards of spelling and usage.

DATE PUBLISHED

DATE READ

MY RATING

WHY I READ THIS BOOK

IT INSPIRED ME TO (READ/LEARN/VISIT)

I WILL RECOMMEND IT TO

BOOK TITLE

AUTHOR

☐ FICTION GENRE

☐ NONFICTION TOPIC

NOTES

MY REVIEW

FINAL TAKEAWAY

You can never get a cup of tea large enough or a book long enough to suit me.

—C. S. Lewis

✧ DATE PUBLISHED ✧

✧ DATE READ ✧

✧ MY RATING ✧

WHY I READ THIS BOOK

IT INSPIRED ME TO (READ/LEARN/VISIT)

I WILL RECOMMEND IT TO

BOOK TITLE

AUTHOR

☐ FICTION GENRE

☐ NONFICTION TOPIC

NOTES

MY REVIEW

FINAL TAKEAWAY

Agatha Christie is the best-selling fiction author, having sold more than 2 billion books.

✧ DATE PUBLISHED ✧

✧ DATE READ ✧

✧ MY RATING ✧

WHY I READ THIS BOOK

IT INSPIRED ME TO (READ/LEARN/VISIT)

I WILL RECOMMEND IT TO

BOOK TITLE

AUTHOR

☐ FICTION GENRE

☐ NONFICTION TOPIC

NOTES

MY REVIEW

FINAL TAKEAWAY

Maybe this is why we read, and why in moments of darkness we return to books: to find words for what we already know.

—Alberto Manguel

DATE PUBLISHED

DATE READ

MY RATING

WHY I READ THIS BOOK

IT INSPIRED ME TO (READ/LEARN/VISIT)

I WILL RECOMMEND IT TO

BOOK TITLE

AUTHOR

☐ FICTION GENRE

☐ NONFICTION TOPIC

NOTES

MY REVIEW

FINAL TAKEAWAY

It wasn't until the twentieth century that books became an integral part of childhood in the developed world.

✧ DATE PUBLISHED ✧

✧ DATE READ ✧

✧ MY RATING ✧

WHY I READ THIS BOOK

IT INSPIRED ME TO (READ/LEARN/VISIT)

I WILL RECOMMEND IT TO

BOOK TITLE

AUTHOR

☐ FICTION GENRE

☐ NONFICTION TOPIC

NOTES

MY REVIEW

FINAL TAKEAWAY

One glance at a book and you hear the voice of another person, perhaps someone dead for thousands of years. To read is to voyage through time.

—Carl Sagan

✧ DATE PUBLISHED ✧

✧ DATE READ ✧

✧ MY RATING ✧

WHY I READ THIS BOOK

IT INSPIRED ME TO (READ/LEARN/VISIT)

I WILL RECOMMEND IT TO

BOOK TITLE

AUTHOR

☐ FICTION GENRE

☐ NONFICTION TOPIC

NOTES

MY REVIEW

FINAL TAKEAWAY

The Holy Land, *created in 1842 by David Roberts and lithographer Louis Haghe, was one of the first mass-produced lithographic books, commencing the rise of mass media.*

✧ DATE PUBLISHED ✧

✧ DATE READ ✧

✧ MY RATING ✧

WHY I READ THIS BOOK

IT INSPIRED ME TO (READ/LEARN/VISIT)

I WILL RECOMMEND IT TO

BOOK TITLE

AUTHOR

☐ FICTION GENRE

☐ NONFICTION TOPIC

NOTES

MY REVIEW

FINAL TAKEAWAY

Today a reader, tomorrow a leader.

—Margaret Fuller

✧ DATE PUBLISHED ✧

✧ DATE READ ✧

✧ MY RATING ✧

WHY I READ THIS BOOK

IT INSPIRED ME TO (READ/LEARN/VISIT)

I WILL RECOMMEND IT TO

BOOK TITLE

AUTHOR

☐ FICTION GENRE

☐ NONFICTION TOPIC

NOTES

MY REVIEW ______________________________

FINAL TAKEAWAY ______________________________

*"It was a dark and stormy night"—
now recognized as the "literary posterchild for bad story starters"—was the opening line to Edward George Bulwer-Lytton's 1830 novel,* Paul Clifford.

DATE PUBLISHED

DATE READ

MY RATING

WHY I READ THIS BOOK

IT INSPIRED ME TO (READ/LEARN/VISIT)

I WILL RECOMMEND IT TO

BOOK TITLE

AUTHOR

☐ FICTION GENRE

☐ NONFICTION TOPIC

NOTES

MY REVIEW

FINAL TAKEAWAY

There is no Frigate like a Book / To take us Lands away.

—Emily Dickinson

DATE PUBLISHED

DATE READ

MY RATING

WHY I READ THIS BOOK

IT INSPIRED ME TO (READ/LEARN/VISIT)

I WILL RECOMMEND IT TO

BOOK TITLE

AUTHOR

☐ FICTION GENRE

☐ NONFICTION TOPIC

NOTES

MY REVIEW

FINAL TAKEAWAY

The award for the longest written sentence goes to Victor Hugo's Les Misérables, *which has one composed of more than 800 words.*

✧ DATE PUBLISHED ✧

✧ DATE READ ✧

✧ MY RATING ✧

WHY I READ THIS BOOK

IT INSPIRED ME TO (READ/LEARN/VISIT)

I WILL RECOMMEND IT TO

BOOK TITLE

AUTHOR

☐ FICTION GENRE

☐ NONFICTION TOPIC

NOTES

MY REVIEW

FINAL TAKEAWAY

I'm old-fashioned and think that reading books is the most glorious pastime that humankind has yet devised.

—Wisława Szymborska

DATE PUBLISHED

DATE READ

MY RATING

WHY I READ THIS BOOK

IT INSPIRED ME TO (READ/LEARN/VISIT)

I WILL RECOMMEND IT TO

BOOK TITLE

AUTHOR

- [ ] FICTION — GENRE
- [ ] NONFICTION — TOPIC

NOTES

MY REVIEW

FINAL TAKEAWAY

Dr. Seuss invented the word "nerd," using it in his 1950 book If I Ran the Zoo.

SHŪSAKU ENDŌ

BIRTH	GENRE	AWARDS
March 27, 1923 *Tokyo, Japan* DEATH *September 29, 1996* *Tokyo, Japan*	*Fiction* POPULAR WORKS Silence, Deep River, White Man	*Akutagawa Prize, Tanizaki Prize, Japanese Order of Culture, Mainichi Cultural Prize, and the Shincho Prize*

WIDELY CONSIDERED one of the greatest Japanese novelists, Shūsaku Endō brought a unique and rare perspective to his novels. Although he was raised in Japan, he converted to Catholicism at the young age of eleven. He studied French literature in Tokyo and French Catholic literature in France before returning to Japan. In the foreword to Endō's *Silence,* Martin Scorsese wrote "Endō himself had great difficulty reconciling his Catholic faith with Japanese culture.... He understood the conflict of faith, the necessity of belief fighting the voice of experience."

Endō's novels often bring the reader face-to-face with complex dilemmas, and explore how the questions and doubts we have can deepen our faith. *Silence*, widely considered to be his masterpiece, looks at seventeenth-century Japan, Jesuit priests, and the decisions between life, death, and faith. Endō seems to be saying that God often speaks loudest in His silence. What does that look like? How do we reconcile this? *Silence* forces the reader to look deeper, like few novels have.

LITERARY MATCHUPS

I PREFER

☐ Fiction	*or*	☐ Nonfiction
☐ Alice	*or*	☐ Dorothy
☐ Biblical Fiction	*or*	☐ Science Fiction
☐ Miss Marple	*or*	☐ Hercule Poirot
☐ Elinor Dashwood	*or*	☐ Marianne Dashwood
☐ Jane Austen	*or*	☐ Charles Dickens
☐ *The Odyssey*	*or*	☐ *The Iliad*
☐ Emily Dickinson	*or*	☐ Ralph Waldo Emerson
☐ *The Great Gatsby*	*or*	☐ *To Kill a Mockingbird*
☐ Shakespeare	*or*	☐ J. K. Rowling

IF I WERE

A CHARACTER IN *LITTLE WOMEN*, I'D BE:

- ☐ Amy
- ☐ Jo
- ☐ Meg
- ☐ Beth

A LITERARY TIME TRAVELER, I'D VISIT:

- ☐ Charles Dickens's London
- ☐ Paul's Rome
- ☐ Mark Twain's Mississippi River
- ☐ Sojourner Truth's New York
- ☐ Martin Luther's Germany
- ☐ C. S. Lewis's Oxford
- ☐ Jane Austen's Derbyshire

PART OF A FAMOUS LITERARY COUPLE, IT WOULD BE:

- ☐ Romeo and Juliet
- ☐ Rhett and Scarlett
- ☐ Elizabeth Bennet and Mr. Darcy
- ☐ Catherine and Heathcliff
- ☐ Sarah and Michael Hosea
- ☐ Aragorn and Arwen

A CHARACTER IN MIDDLE EARTH, I'D BE:

- ☐ Gandalf
- ☐ Aragorn
- ☐ Gimli
- ☐ Éowyn
- ☐ Frodo
- ☐ Sam

A LITERARY VILLAIN, I'D BE:

- ☐ Professor Moriarty
- ☐ Sauron
- ☐ Count Dracula
- ☐ The White Witch
- ☐ Lord Voldemort

A CHARACTER IN *THE PILGRIM'S PROGRESS*, I'D BE:

- ☐ Obstinate
- ☐ Mr. Worldly Wiseman
- ☐ Pliable
- ☐ Mr. Legality
- ☐ Faithful
- ☐ Talkative

MY FAVORITE QUOTES

✧ DATE PUBLISHED ✧

✧ DATE READ ✧

✧ MY RATING ✧

WHY I READ THIS BOOK

IT INSPIRED ME TO (READ/LEARN/VISIT)

I WILL RECOMMEND IT TO

BOOK TITLE

AUTHOR

☐ FICTION GENRE

☐ NONFICTION TOPIC

NOTES

MY REVIEW

FINAL TAKEAWAY

Never trust anyone who has not brought a book with them.

—Lemony Snicket

DATE PUBLISHED

DATE READ

MY RATING

WHY I READ THIS BOOK

IT INSPIRED ME TO (READ/LEARN/VISIT)

I WILL RECOMMEND IT TO

BOOK TITLE

AUTHOR

☐ FICTION GENRE

☐ NONFICTION TOPIC

NOTES

MY REVIEW

FINAL TAKEAWAY

Cervantes's Don Quixote, *published in 1605, is considered to be the first modern novel, but the novel as a genre didn't become popular until the 1800s.*

✧ DATE PUBLISHED ✧

✧ DATE READ ✧

✧ MY RATING ✧

WHY I READ THIS BOOK

IT INSPIRED ME TO (READ/LEARN/VISIT)

I WILL RECOMMEND IT TO

BOOK TITLE

AUTHOR

☐ FICTION GENRE

☐ NONFICTION TOPIC

NOTES

MY REVIEW

FINAL TAKEAWAY

"Classic"—a book which people praise and don't read.

—Mark Twain

BOOK TITLE

AUTHOR

☐ FICTION GENRE

☐ NONFICTION TOPIC

NOTES

DATE PUBLISHED

DATE READ

MY RATING

WHY I READ THIS BOOK

IT INSPIRED ME TO (READ/LEARN/VISIT)

I WILL RECOMMEND IT TO

MY REVIEW

FINAL TAKEAWAY

Nature author Rachel Carson's 1962 book, Silent Spring, *sparked the environmental movement and led to the ban of the dangerous pesticide DDT.*

DATE PUBLISHED
DATE READ
MY RATING
WHY I READ THIS BOOK
IT INSPIRED ME TO (READ/LEARN/VISIT)
I WILL RECOMMEND IT TO
BOOK TITLE
AUTHOR
FICTION
NONFICTION
GENRE
TOPIC
NOTES

MY REVIEW ____________________

FINAL TAKEAWAY ____________________

Books are the quietest and most constant of friends; they are the most accessible and wisest of counselors, and the most patient of teachers.

—Charles W. Eliot

✧ DATE PUBLISHED ✧

✧ DATE READ ✧

✧ MY RATING ✧

WHY I READ THIS BOOK

IT INSPIRED ME TO (READ/LEARN/VISIT)

I WILL RECOMMEND IT TO

BOOK TITLE

AUTHOR

☐ FICTION GENRE

☐ NONFICTION TOPIC

NOTES

MY REVIEW ____

FINAL TAKEAWAY ____

The phrase "cool as a cucumber" first appeared in John Gay's poem "A New Song of New Similies" in 1732.

✧ DATE PUBLISHED ✧

✧ DATE READ ✧

✧ MY RATING ✧

WHY I READ THIS BOOK

IT INSPIRED ME TO (READ/LEARN/VISIT)

I WILL RECOMMEND IT TO

BOOK TITLE

AUTHOR

☐ FICTION GENRE

☐ NONFICTION TOPIC

NOTES

MY REVIEW

FINAL TAKEAWAY

The only thing you absolutely have to know is the location of the library.

—Albert Einstein

DATE PUBLISHED

DATE READ

MY RATING

WHY I READ THIS BOOK

IT INSPIRED ME TO (READ/LEARN/VISIT)

I WILL RECOMMEND IT TO

BOOK TITLE

AUTHOR

☐ FICTION GENRE

☐ NONFICTION TOPIC

NOTES

MY REVIEW

FINAL TAKEAWAY

The title character of Alice's Adventures in Wonderland *was based on a real ten-year-old girl.*

✧ DATE PUBLISHED ✧

✧ DATE READ ✧

✧ MY RATING ✧

WHY I READ THIS BOOK

IT INSPIRED ME TO (READ/LEARN/VISIT)

I WILL RECOMMEND IT TO

BOOK TITLE

AUTHOR

☐ FICTION GENRE

☐ NONFICTION TOPIC

NOTES

MY REVIEW

FINAL TAKEAWAY

Do not read, as children do, to amuse yourself,
or like the ambitious, for the purpose of instruction.
No, read in order to live.

—Gustave Flaubert

✧ DATE PUBLISHED ✧

✧ DATE READ ✧

✧ MY RATING ✧

WHY I READ THIS BOOK

IT INSPIRED ME TO (READ/LEARN/VISIT)

I WILL RECOMMEND IT TO

BOOK TITLE

AUTHOR

☐ FICTION GENRE

☐ NONFICTION TOPIC

NOTES

MY REVIEW

FINAL TAKEAWAY

At the time of publication in the 1850s, Harriet Beecher Stowe's Uncle Tom's Cabin *was outsold only by the Bible.*

✧ DATE PUBLISHED ✧

✧ DATE READ ✧

✧ MY RATING ✧

WHY I READ THIS BOOK

IT INSPIRED ME TO (READ/LEARN/VISIT)

I WILL RECOMMEND IT TO

BOOK TITLE

AUTHOR

☐ FICTION GENRE

☐ NONFICTION TOPIC

NOTES

MY REVIEW

FINAL TAKEAWAY

My alma mater was books, a good library.... I could spend the rest of my life reading, just satisfying my curiosity.

—Malcolm X

DATE PUBLISHED

DATE READ

MY RATING

WHY I READ THIS BOOK

IT INSPIRED ME TO (READ/LEARN/VISIT)

I WILL RECOMMEND IT TO

BOOK TITLE

AUTHOR

☐ FICTION GENRE

☐ NONFICTION TOPIC

NOTES

MY REVIEW

FINAL TAKEAWAY

The Nuremberg Chronicle *(1493) presents world history from a biblical and classical perspective and was a printing marvel, illustrated with more than 1,800 woodcuts.*

DATE PUBLISHED

DATE READ

MY RATING

WHY I READ THIS BOOK

IT INSPIRED ME TO (READ/LEARN/VISIT)

I WILL RECOMMEND IT TO

BOOK TITLE

AUTHOR

☐ FICTION GENRE

☐ NONFICTION TOPIC

NOTES

MY REVIEW

FINAL TAKEAWAY

Reading brings us unknown friends.

—Honoré de Balzac

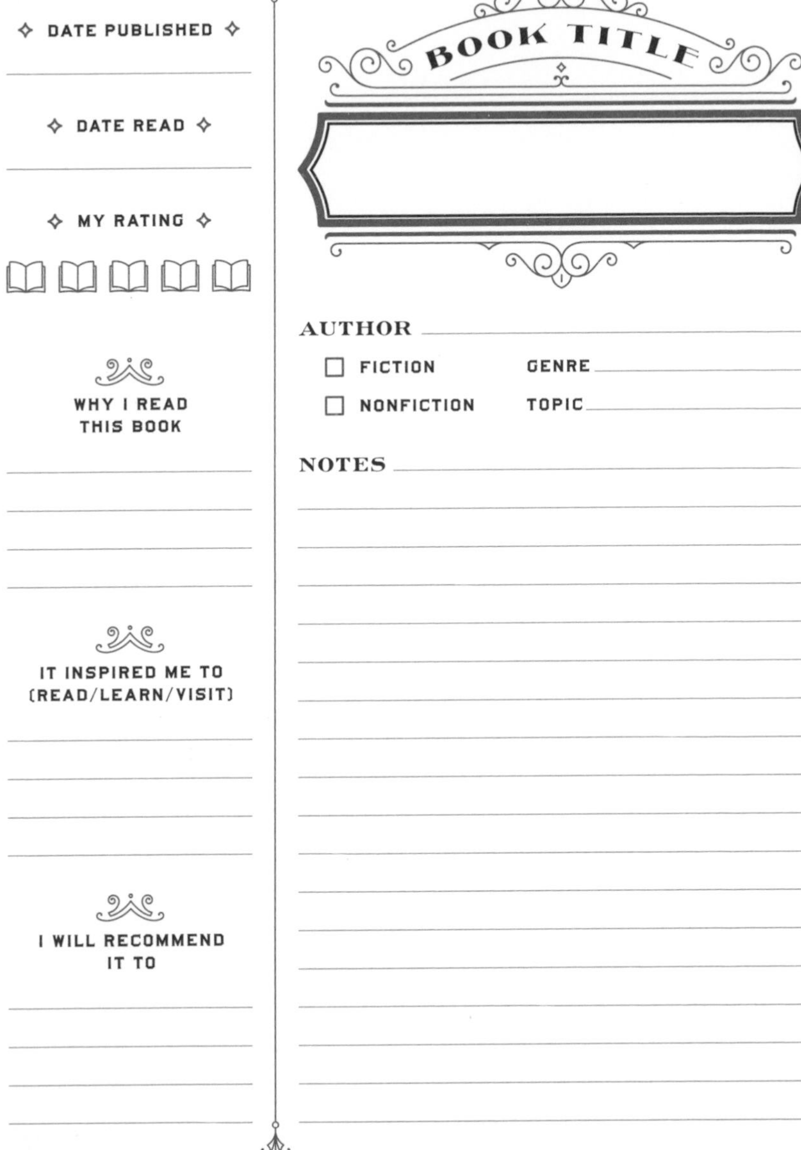
DATE PUBLISHED
DATE READ
MY RATING
WHY I READ THIS BOOK
IT INSPIRED ME TO (READ/LEARN/VISIT)
I WILL RECOMMEND IT TO
BOOK TITLE
AUTHOR
FICTION
NONFICTION
GENRE
TOPIC
NOTES

MY REVIEW ______

FINAL TAKEAWAY ______

The first American fairy tale is considered to be L. Frank Baum's The Wonderful Wizard of Oz *(1900).*

✧ DATE PUBLISHED ✧

✧ DATE READ ✧

✧ MY RATING ✧

WHY I READ THIS BOOK

IT INSPIRED ME TO (READ/LEARN/VISIT)

I WILL RECOMMEND IT TO

BOOK TITLE

AUTHOR

☐ FICTION GENRE

☐ NONFICTION TOPIC

NOTES

MY REVIEW

FINAL TAKEAWAY

Books are not made for furniture, but there is nothing else that so beautifully furnishes a house.

—Henry Ward Beecher

FREDERICK DOUGLASS

BIRTH
c. February 14, 1818
Cordova, Maryland

DEATH
February 20, 1895
Washington, DC

POPULAR WORKS
Narrative of the Life of Frederick Douglass, an American Slave; My Bondage and My Freedom

GENRE
Nonfiction

AWARDS
National Historic Site in Washington, DC

FROM AN EARLY AGE, Frederick Douglass recognized the inherent power of words. Born into slavery, he secretly taught himself to read and write, even while knowing the punishment was death. Many of his books, including the *Narrative of the Life of Frederick Douglass*, are full of philosophical questions. Perplexing questions. Hard questions. Calling on people and the church, Douglass wrote in *Narrative*, "It was not color, but crime, not God, but man, that afforded the true explanation of the existence of slavery; nor was I long in finding out another important truth...what man can make, man can unmake."

He agitated society because he saw how the teachings of Christ contrasted drastically to what he endured. One of his most famous quotes from *Narrative* reads, "I love the pure, peaceable, and impartial Christianity of Christ: I therefore hate the corrupt, slave-holding, women-whipping, cradle-plundering, partial and hypocritical Christianity of this land. Indeed, I see no reason, but the most deceitful one, for calling this religion of this land Christianity. I look upon it as the climax of all misnomers, the boldest of all frauds, and the grossest of all libels."

In the 1969 introduction to Douglass's *My Bondage and My Freedom*, Philip S. Foner sums up Douglass's impact: "Although written over a century ago, the autobiography is completely meaningful today. It is not only the story of a black man who experienced slavery and escaped from it, but of a human being who devoted his life in freedom to help his own people and others achieve freedom."

A GUIDE TO BOOKISH HOLIDAYS

Winnie the Pooh Day	*January 18*
Library Lovers' Day	*February 14*
Read Across America	*March 2*
World Book Day	*March 5*
World Poetry Day	*March 21*
Tolkien Reading Day	*March 25*
Children's Book Day	*April 2*
National Library Week	*April*
World Book and Copyright Day	*April 23*
Tell a Story Day	*April 27*
International Inklings Day	*May 11*
Paperback Book Day	*July 30*
Book Lovers Day	*August 9*
Read a Book Day	*September 6*
International Literacy Day	*September 8*
Banned Books Week	*Last week of September*
National Book Month	*October*
Author's Day	*November 1*
National Family Literacy Day	*November 1*
National Novel Writing Month	*November*
Picture Book Month	*November*

BOOK TALK

DISCUSSION QUESTIONS AND CONVERSATION STARTERS

- What was your favorite quote or passage?
- Which character did you relate to the most? What do you think inspired the connection?
- How did you feel about the ending? Is there anything you would have changed?
- How did the book influence your perspective or worldview?
- In what ways did God speak to you through this book?
- If you could have witnessed any of the scenes firsthand, which one would you choose and why?
- What most surprised you?
- If you could ask the author one question about the book, what would it be?
- Were there any passages or characters you struggled with? Was there anything about the book that angered or frustrated you?
- Does this book remind you of any others you've read?
- If this book were made into a movie, what features would you most want the filmmakers to get right? If it has already been adapted into a movie, what do you think should have been done differently?
- Would you recommend this book to others? Why or why not?
- Which character or person in the story would you want to have dinner with?
- Would you read other books by this author? Why or why not?
- If you had to come up with another title for this book, what would it be?
- How did you feel about the writing quality and style of the book? Was it easy to understand? Fast-paced? Too wordy?
- What is your opinion of the narrator? Do you think he or she was trustworthy?
- What topics did the book inspire you to learn more about?
- How did this book deepen or otherwise affect your faith?

BOOKS ON SCREEN

BEST MOVIE ADAPTATIONS OF BOOKS

WORST MOVIE ADAPTATIONS OF BOOKS

BOOK I'D MOST WANT TO MAKE INTO A MOVIE

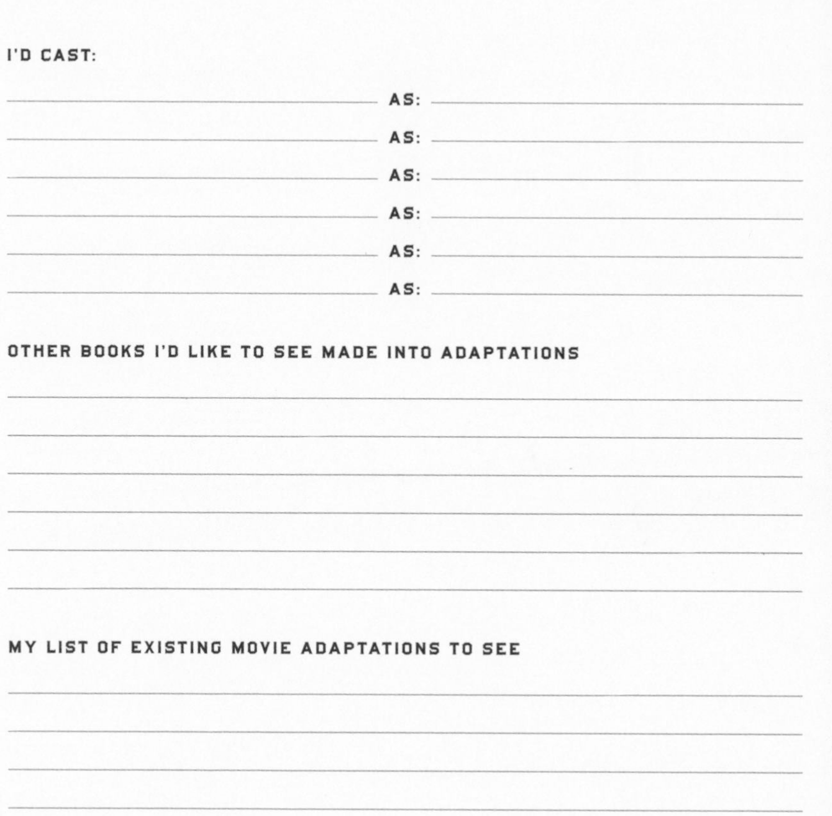

I'D CAST:

AS:

AS:

AS:

AS:

AS:

AS:

OTHER BOOKS I'D LIKE TO SEE MADE INTO ADAPTATIONS

MY LIST OF EXISTING MOVIE ADAPTATIONS TO SEE

DATE PUBLISHED

DATE READ

MY RATING

WHY I READ THIS BOOK

IT INSPIRED ME TO (READ/LEARN/VISIT)

I WILL RECOMMEND IT TO

BOOK TITLE

AUTHOR

☐ FICTION GENRE

☐ NONFICTION TOPIC

NOTES

MY REVIEW

FINAL TAKEAWAY

Aesop—if he truly existed—is thought to have been a Greek-speaking slave. His stories, passed down by oral tradition as early as the fourth century BCE, were first published as Esopus *in Germany circa 1476.*

✧ DATE PUBLISHED ✧

✧ DATE READ ✧

✧ MY RATING ✧

WHY I READ THIS BOOK

IT INSPIRED ME TO (READ/LEARN/VISIT)

I WILL RECOMMEND IT TO

BOOK TITLE

AUTHOR

☐ FICTION GENRE

☐ NONFICTION TOPIC

NOTES

MY REVIEW

FINAL TAKEAWAY

There is more treasure in books than in all the pirate's loot on Treasure Island.

—Walt Disney

DATE PUBLISHED

DATE READ

MY RATING

WHY I READ THIS BOOK

IT INSPIRED ME TO (READ/LEARN/VISIT)

I WILL RECOMMEND IT TO

BOOK TITLE

AUTHOR

☐ FICTION GENRE

☐ NONFICTION TOPIC

NOTES

MY REVIEW

FINAL TAKEAWAY

Harry Potter and the Deathly Hallows *had an initial print run of 12 million copies, the largest in history.*

✧ DATE PUBLISHED ✧

✧ DATE READ ✧

✧ MY RATING ✧

WHY I READ THIS BOOK

IT INSPIRED ME TO (READ/LEARN/VISIT)

I WILL RECOMMEND IT TO

BOOK TITLE

AUTHOR

☐ FICTION GENRE

☐ NONFICTION TOPIC

NOTES

MY REVIEW

FINAL TAKEAWAY

To learn to read is to light a fire; every syllable that is spelled out is a spark.

—Victor Hugo

DATE PUBLISHED

DATE READ

MY RATING

WHY I READ THIS BOOK

IT INSPIRED ME TO (READ/LEARN/VISIT)

I WILL RECOMMEND IT TO

BOOK TITLE

AUTHOR

☐ FICTION GENRE

☐ NONFICTION TOPIC

NOTES

MY REVIEW

FINAL TAKEAWAY

Author names didn't use to be included on book covers, since covers were considered to be works of art.

DATE PUBLISHED

DATE READ

MY RATING

WHY I READ THIS BOOK

IT INSPIRED ME TO (READ/LEARN/VISIT)

I WILL RECOMMEND IT TO

BOOK TITLE

AUTHOR

☐ FICTION GENRE

☐ NONFICTION TOPIC

NOTES

MY REVIEW

FINAL TAKEAWAY

Until I feared I would lose it, I never loved to read.
One does not love breathing.

—Harper Lee

✧ DATE PUBLISHED ✧

✧ DATE READ ✧

✧ MY RATING ✧

WHY I READ THIS BOOK

IT INSPIRED ME TO (READ/LEARN/VISIT)

I WILL RECOMMEND IT TO

BOOK TITLE

AUTHOR

☐ FICTION GENRE

☐ NONFICTION TOPIC

NOTES

MY REVIEW

FINAL TAKEAWAY

Before printed books, writers were usually anonymous scribes who had to copy words by hand rather than create original work.

✧ DATE PUBLISHED ✧

✧ DATE READ ✧

✧ MY RATING ✧

WHY I READ THIS BOOK

IT INSPIRED ME TO (READ/LEARN/VISIT)

I WILL RECOMMEND IT TO

BOOK TITLE

AUTHOR

☐ FICTION GENRE

☐ NONFICTION TOPIC

NOTES

MY REVIEW

FINAL TAKEAWAY

I find television very educating. Every time somebody turns on the set, I go into the other room and read a book.

—Groucho Marx

DATE PUBLISHED
DATE READ
MY RATING
WHY I READ THIS BOOK
IT INSPIRED ME TO (READ/LEARN/VISIT)
I WILL RECOMMEND IT TO
BOOK TITLE
AUTHOR
FICTION
NONFICTION
GENRE
TOPIC
NOTES

MY REVIEW

FINAL TAKEAWAY

The Bay Psalm Book, *a translation of the Book of Psalms for the Christian dissenters who settled in Plymouth, Massachusetts, was the first book printed in British North America (in 1640).*

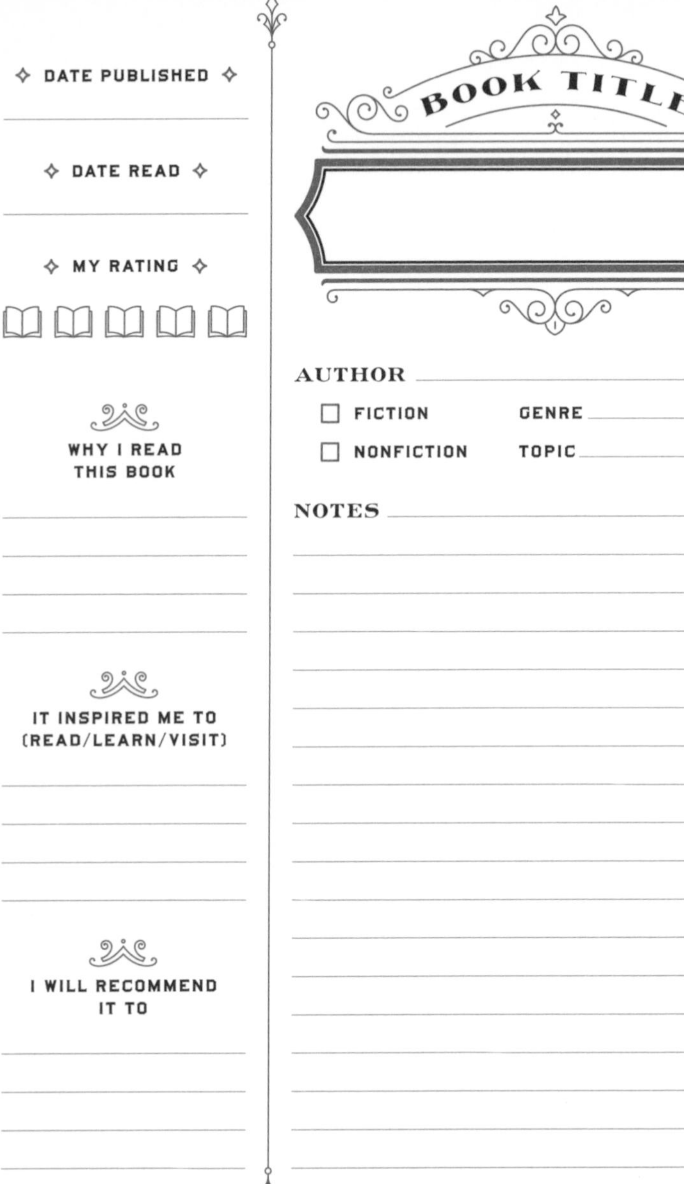
DATE PUBLISHED
DATE READ
MY RATING
WHY I READ THIS BOOK
IT INSPIRED ME TO (READ/LEARN/VISIT)
I WILL RECOMMEND IT TO
BOOK TITLE
AUTHOR
FICTION
NONFICTION
GENRE
TOPIC
NOTES

MY REVIEW

FINAL TAKEAWAY

I do believe something very magical can happen when you read a good book.

—J. K. Rowling

DATE PUBLISHED

DATE READ

MY RATING

WHY I READ THIS BOOK

IT INSPIRED ME TO (READ/LEARN/VISIT)

I WILL RECOMMEND IT TO

BOOK TITLE

AUTHOR

☐ FICTION GENRE

☐ NONFICTION TOPIC

NOTES

MY REVIEW ____________________

FINAL TAKEAWAY ____________________

The phrase "don't judge a book by its cover" probably originated in the 1944 edition of the African journal American Speech*: "You can't judge a book by its binding."*

DATE PUBLISHED

DATE READ

MY RATING

WHY I READ THIS BOOK

IT INSPIRED ME TO (READ/LEARN/VISIT)

I WILL RECOMMEND IT TO

BOOK TITLE

AUTHOR

☐ FICTION GENRE

☐ NONFICTION TOPIC

NOTES

MY REVIEW ________________________________

FINAL TAKEAWAY ________________________________

That's the thing about books. They let you travel without moving your feet.

—Jhumpa Lahiri

DATE PUBLISHED

DATE READ

MY RATING

WHY I READ THIS BOOK

IT INSPIRED ME TO (READ/LEARN/VISIT)

I WILL RECOMMEND IT TO

BOOK TITLE

AUTHOR

☐ FICTION GENRE

☐ NONFICTION TOPIC

NOTES

MY REVIEW

FINAL TAKEAWAY

Peterborough Town Library in New Hampshire was the first tax-supported public library in the world.

DATE PUBLISHED

DATE READ

MY RATING

WHY I READ THIS BOOK

IT INSPIRED ME TO (READ/LEARN/VISIT)

I WILL RECOMMEND IT TO

BOOK TITLE

AUTHOR

- [ ] FICTION GENRE
- [ ] NONFICTION TOPIC

NOTES

MY REVIEW ______________________________

FINAL TAKEAWAY ______________________________

There is no friend as loyal as a book.

—Ernest Hemingway

DATE PUBLISHED

DATE READ

MY RATING

WHY I READ THIS BOOK

IT INSPIRED ME TO (READ/LEARN/VISIT)

I WILL RECOMMEND IT TO

BOOK TITLE

AUTHOR

☐ FICTION GENRE

☐ NONFICTION TOPIC

NOTES

MY REVIEW

FINAL TAKEAWAY

Prior to 1535, titles weren't printed on book spines, so books were shelved backward with the edges of the pages facing out.

DOROTHY SAYERS

BIRTH
June 13, 1893
Oxford, United Kingdom

DEATH
December 17, 1957
Witham, United Kingdom

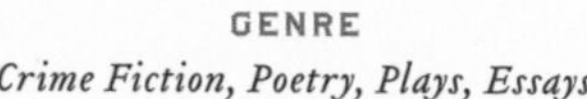

GENRE
Crime Fiction, Poetry, Plays, Essays

POPULAR WORKS
Whose Body?, Gaudy Night, Busman's Honeymoon, The Man Born to Be King

DOROTHY SAYERS was a hard worker throughout her life living by her personal credo, "The only Christian work is good work, well done." Although she is best known for her crime fiction, Sayers was a prolific writer whose carefully researched and diverse works included poetry, plays, essays, short stories, and translations. Sayers was the only daughter of a clergyman and headmaster. From an early age, she showed a remarkable gift for languages, learning Latin and French by the age of seven. After attending boarding school, she won a scholarship in 1912 to the Oxford women's college, where she studied modern languages and medieval literature. She went on to earn her master's from Oxford University in 1920, becoming one of the first women to receive a degree.

Before writing full-time, Sayers worked for the Oxford publisher Blackwell's, taught English in Normandy, and spent nine years as a copywriter at an advertising firm. A passionate Anglican, she wrote many theological essays, but her most provocative work was her play *The Man Born to Be King*, in which she portrayed Christ speaking modern English. Though controversial, it revolutionized religious play-writing. Undaunted by opposition, she proved willing to engage in intellectual debate, particularly regarding work, theology, and the role of women. She urged Christians to engage with difficult questions and to reject a watered-down version of Jesus. Never one to promote a religious agenda, Dorothy Sayers nevertheless had a profound influence on modern Christianity because she willingly challenged the pious preconceptions of her time.

MY PERSONAL FAVORITES

FAVORITE BOOKS

FAVORITE AUTHORS

FAVORITE CHRISTIAN LIVING BOOKS

FAVORITE BIOGRAPHIES / MEMOIRS

MY FAVORITE PLACES TO READ

(check all that apply)

- ☐ at home
- ☐ in a coffee shop
- ☐ at the beach
- ☐ in bed
- ☐ on an airplane
- ☐ at the library

MY FAVORITE GENRES

(check all that apply)

- ☐ graphic novel
- ☐ classic
- ☐ adventure
- ☐ biography / autobiography / memoir
- ☐ contemporary fiction
- ☐ horror
- ☐ historical fiction
- ☐ drama / play
- ☐ humor
- ☐ mystery / crime
- ☐ romance
- ☐ science fiction
- ☐ travel

WHO WROTE IT?

Match the Quote to Its Source: *Choose the author who wrote the quote by writing the letter next to the quote. If you get stuck, you'll find the answer key on page 206.*

QUOTE

1 ___ "He stepped down, trying not to look long at her, as if she were the sun, yet he saw her, like the sun, even without looking."

2 ___ "Behind every exquisite thing that existed, there was something tragic."

3 ___ "You never really understand a person until you consider things from his point of view.... Until you climb inside of his skin and walk around in it."

4 ___ "To thine own self be true, and it must follow, as the night the day, thou canst not then be false to any man."

5 ___ "As he read, I fell in love the way you fall asleep: slowly, and then all at once."

6 ___ "It is a truth universally acknowledged, that a single man in possession of a good fortune, must be in want of a wife."

7 ___ "Wherever you fly, you'll be best of the best. / Wherever you go, you will top all the rest."

8 ___ "There is no greater agony than bearing an untold story inside you."

9 ___ "Grown-ups never understand anything by themselves, and it is tiresome for children to be always and forever explaining things to them."

10 ___ "Get busy living or get busy dying."

11 ___ "All that is gold does not glitter, / Not all those who wander are lost."

12 ___ "You are your best thing."

13 ___ "It was the best of times, it was the worst of times, it was the age of wisdom, it was the age of foolishness, it was the epoch of belief, it was the epoch of incredulity."

14 ___ "And so we beat on, boats against the current, borne back ceaselessly into the past."

15 ___ "It was a bright cold day in April, and the clocks were striking thirteen."

A John Green, *The Fault in Our Stars*

B Harper Lee, *To Kill a Mockingbird*

C Leo Tolstoy, *Anna Karenina*

D George Orwell, *1984*

E Antoine de Saint-Exupéry, *The Little Prince*

F Dr. Seuss, *Oh, The Places You'll Go!*

G Toni Morrison, *Beloved*

H J.R.R. Tolkien, *The Lord of the Rings*

I Stephen King, *Rita Hayworth and the Shawshank Redemption*

J Maya Angelou, *I Know Why the Caged Bird Sings*

K Charles Dickens, *A Tale of Two Cities*

L Jane Austen, *Pride and Prejudice*

M F. Scott Fitzgerald, *The Great Gatsby*

N Oscar Wilde, *The Picture of Dorian Gray*

O William Shakespeare, *Hamlet*

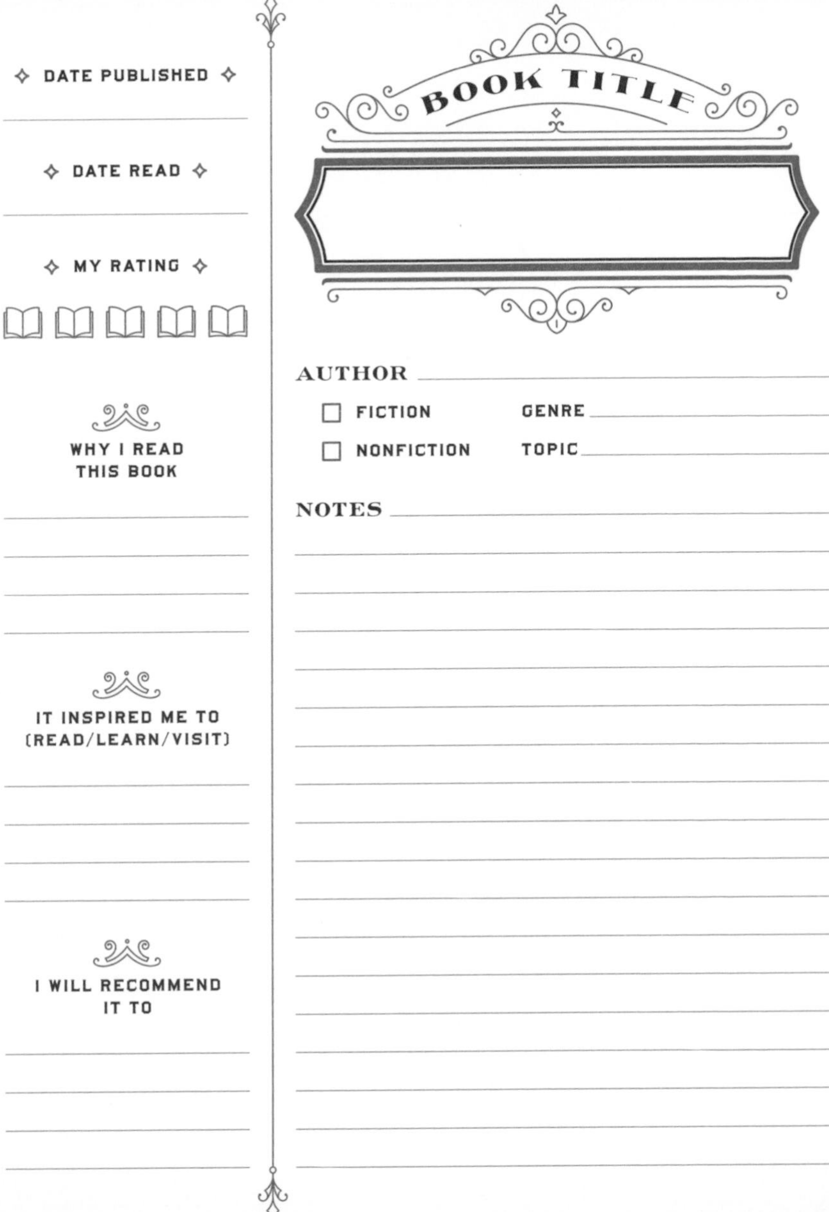
DATE PUBLISHED
DATE READ
MY RATING
WHY I READ THIS BOOK
IT INSPIRED ME TO (READ/LEARN/VISIT)
I WILL RECOMMEND IT TO
BOOK TITLE
AUTHOR
FICTION
NONFICTION
GENRE
TOPIC
NOTES

MY REVIEW

FINAL TAKEAWAY

Reading is a form of prayer, a guided meditation that briefly makes us believe we're someone else, disrupting the delusion that we're permanent and at the center of the universe.

—George Saunders

✧ DATE PUBLISHED ✧

✧ DATE READ ✧

✧ MY RATING ✧

WHY I READ THIS BOOK

IT INSPIRED ME TO (READ/LEARN/VISIT)

I WILL RECOMMEND IT TO

BOOK TITLE

AUTHOR

☐ FICTION GENRE

☐ NONFICTION TOPIC

NOTES

MY REVIEW

FINAL TAKEAWAY

Books that were penned or conceived behind bars include Don Quixote *by Miguel de Cervantes,* Pilgrim's Progress *by John Bunyan, and* De Profundis *by Oscar Wilde.*

✧ DATE PUBLISHED ✧

✧ DATE READ ✧

✧ MY RATING ✧

WHY I READ THIS BOOK

IT INSPIRED ME TO (READ/LEARN/VISIT)

I WILL RECOMMEND IT TO

BOOK TITLE

AUTHOR

☐ FICTION GENRE

☐ NONFICTION TOPIC

NOTES

MY REVIEW

FINAL TAKEAWAY

Reading gives us someplace to go when we have to stay where we are.

—Mason Cooley

DATE PUBLISHED

DATE READ

MY RATING

WHY I READ THIS BOOK

IT INSPIRED ME TO (READ/LEARN/VISIT)

I WILL RECOMMEND IT TO

BOOK TITLE

AUTHOR

- [ ] FICTION
- [ ] NONFICTION

GENRE

TOPIC

NOTES

MY REVIEW ______________________________

FINAL TAKEAWAY ______________________________

Virginia Woolf wrote most of her books while standing.

DATE PUBLISHED

DATE READ

MY RATING

WHY I READ THIS BOOK

IT INSPIRED ME TO (READ/LEARN/VISIT)

I WILL RECOMMEND IT TO

BOOK TITLE

AUTHOR

☐ FICTION GENRE

☐ NONFICTION TOPIC

NOTES

MY REVIEW

FINAL TAKEAWAY

Books are a uniquely portable magic.

—Stephen King

DATE PUBLISHED

DATE READ

MY RATING

WHY I READ THIS BOOK

IT INSPIRED ME TO (READ/LEARN/VISIT)

I WILL RECOMMEND IT TO

BOOK TITLE

AUTHOR

☐ FICTION GENRE

☐ NONFICTION TOPIC

NOTES

MY REVIEW

FINAL TAKEAWAY

Alice Brown's Fools of Nature *(1887) was the first book to be considered a bestseller.*

DATE PUBLISHED

DATE READ

MY RATING

WHY I READ THIS BOOK

IT INSPIRED ME TO (READ/LEARN/VISIT)

I WILL RECOMMEND IT TO

BOOK TITLE

AUTHOR

☐ FICTION GENRE

☐ NONFICTION TOPIC

NOTES

MY REVIEW

FINAL TAKEAWAY

The person who deserves most pity is a lonesome one on a rainy day who doesn't know how to read.

—Benjamin Franklin

DATE PUBLISHED
DATE READ
MY RATING
WHY I READ THIS BOOK
IT INSPIRED ME TO (READ/LEARN/VISIT)
I WILL RECOMMEND IT TO
BOOK TITLE
AUTHOR
FICTION
GENRE
NONFICTION
TOPIC
NOTES

MY REVIEW

FINAL TAKEAWAY

Women buy 68 percent of all books sold.

DATE PUBLISHED

DATE READ

MY RATING

WHY I READ THIS BOOK

IT INSPIRED ME TO (READ/LEARN/VISIT)

I WILL RECOMMEND IT TO

BOOK TITLE

AUTHOR

FICTION

NONFICTION

GENRE

TOPIC

NOTES

MY REVIEW

FINAL TAKEAWAY

There are many little ways to enlarge your child's world.
Love of books is the best of all.

—Jacqueline Kennedy Onassis

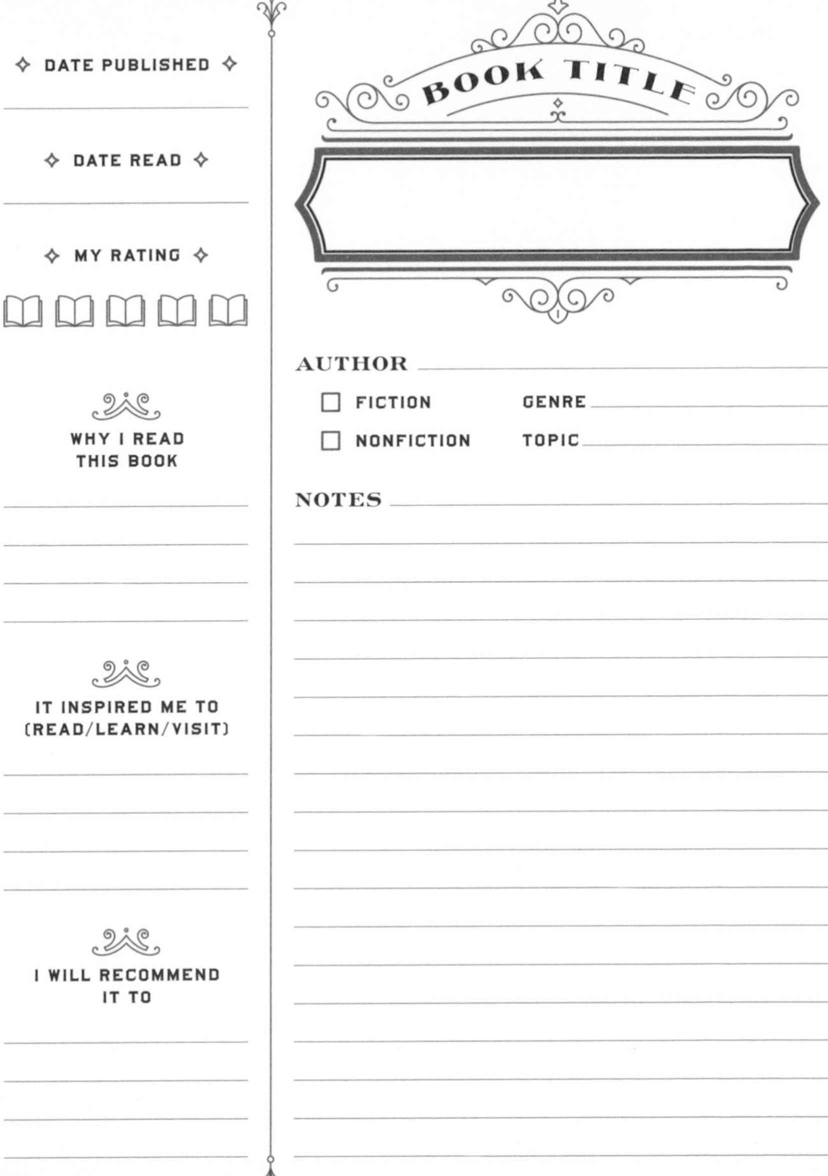
DATE PUBLISHED
DATE READ
MY RATING
WHY I READ THIS BOOK
IT INSPIRED ME TO (READ/LEARN/VISIT)
I WILL RECOMMEND IT TO
BOOK TITLE
AUTHOR
FICTION
NONFICTION
GENRE
TOPIC
NOTES

MY REVIEW

FINAL TAKEAWAY

The term "bookworm" derives from tiny insects that feed on the binding of books.

✧ DATE PUBLISHED ✧

✧ DATE READ ✧

✧ MY RATING ✧

WHY I READ THIS BOOK

IT INSPIRED ME TO (READ/LEARN/VISIT)

I WILL RECOMMEND IT TO

BOOK TITLE

AUTHOR

☐ FICTION GENRE

☐ NONFICTION TOPIC

NOTES

MY REVIEW

FINAL TAKEAWAY

Reading is a conversation. All books talk.
But a good book listens as well.

—Mark Haddon

DATE PUBLISHED

DATE READ

MY RATING

WHY I READ THIS BOOK

IT INSPIRED ME TO (READ/LEARN/VISIT)

I WILL RECOMMEND IT TO

BOOK TITLE

AUTHOR

☐ FICTION GENRE

☐ NONFICTION TOPIC

NOTES

MY REVIEW ______________________________

FINAL TAKEAWAY ______________________________

A 2013 study conducted by Rush University Medical Center in Chicago discovered that consistent readers tend to show fewer signs of memory loss as they age.

✧ DATE PUBLISHED ✧

✧ DATE READ ✧

✧ MY RATING ✧

WHY I READ THIS BOOK

IT INSPIRED ME TO (READ/LEARN/VISIT)

I WILL RECOMMEND IT TO

BOOK TITLE

AUTHOR

☐ FICTION GENRE

☐ NONFICTION TOPIC

NOTES

MY REVIEW

FINAL TAKEAWAY

Reading makes immigrants of us all. It takes us away from home, but more important, it finds homes for us everywhere.

—Jean Rhys

BOOK TITLE
DATE PUBLISHED
DATE READ
MY RATING
WHY I READ THIS BOOK
IT INSPIRED ME TO (READ/LEARN/VISIT)
I WILL RECOMMEND IT TO
AUTHOR
FICTION
NONFICTION
GENRE
TOPIC
NOTES

MY REVIEW

FINAL TAKEAWAY

More commonly known for his heart-wrenching tragedies and plucky comedies, William Shakespeare can also be thanked for adding some 1,600 words to the English language, such as belongings, addiction, fashionable, *and* swagger.

DATE PUBLISHED
DATE READ
MY RATING
WHY I READ THIS BOOK
IT INSPIRED ME TO (READ/LEARN/VISIT)
I WILL RECOMMEND IT TO
BOOK TITLE
AUTHOR
FICTION
NONFICTION
GENRE
TOPIC
NOTES

MY REVIEW

FINAL TAKEAWAY

In the end, we'll all become stories.

—Margaret Atwood

RICHARD TWISS

BIRTH	DEATH	POPULAR WORKS
June 11, 1954 *Rosebud Indian Reservation, South Dakota*	*February 9, 2013* *Washington, DC* GENRE *Theology*	Rescuing the Gospel from the Cowboys, One Church Many Tribes, Dancing Our Prayers

RICHARD TWISS, author, ordained pastor, and beloved speaker, was not one to take the conventional approach when it came to sharing the gospel of Jesus. As he explained it, "I am a follower of Jesus, though I would not call myself a Christian." Even so, his legacy of faith and racial reconciliation seems to be all the stronger because of his unique message and testimony.

As a young man, Twiss despised what he viewed as "white man's religion" and explored everything from Hinduism to Buddhism. It wasn't until a particular low point during a drug overdose in Hawaii that he uttered his first genuine—if not completely faith-filled—prayer. Immediately, he experienced an overwhelming sense of peace, and from that moment, he began to embrace the way of Jesus.

But accepting Jesus did not mean forsaking his Sicangu Lakota Oyate heritage. Claiming the truth that God loves and accepts everyone regardless of background, culture, or traditional practices, Twiss made it his dream "to inspire a cultural revitalization within a redemptive biblical framework." In 1997, he and his wife founded Wiconi International, named after the Lakota word for *life*, with the mission of fostering racial reconciliation and building community between First Nations people and other sectors of Americans.

In 2013, Richard Twiss suffered a fatal heart attack while in Washington, DC, for the National Prayer Breakfast. His life remains a testament of fervent faith and unwavering passion in sharing the way of Jesus with all nations.

100 INSPIRING BOOKS TO SHAPE YOUR FAITH

This list covers books from a wide range of Christian viewpoints. Engaging with them will not only shape your faith, but also cultivate informed discussions with others.

NONFICTION

- ☐ *My Utmost for His Highest* by Oswald Chambers (1935)
- ☐ *Mere Christianity* by C. S. Lewis (1952)
- ☐ *Knowing God* by J. I. Packer (1973)
- ☐ *The Holiness of God* by R. C. Sproul (1985)
- ☐ *The Christian's Secret of a Happy Life* by Hannah Whitall Smith (1875)
- ☐ *The Imitation of Christ* by Thomas à Kempis (1418–1427)
- ☐ *Basic Christianity* by John Stott (1958)
- ☐ *Crazy Love* by Francis Chan (2008)
- ☐ *The Reason for God* by Timothy Keller (2008)
- ☐ *Radical* by David Platt (2010)
- ☐ *The Pursuit of God* by A. W. Tozer (1948)
- ☐ *The Purpose Driven Life* by Rick Warren (2002)
- ☐ *The Case for Christ* by Lee Strobel (1998)
- ☐ *Learning to Walk in the Dark* by Barbara Brown Taylor (2015)
- ☐ *The Practice of the Presence of God* by Brother Lawrence (1693)
- ☐ *A Long Obedience in the Same Direction* by Eugene H. Peterson (1980)
- ☐ *The Divine Conspiracy* by Dallas Willard (1998)
- ☐ *Life of the Beloved* by Henri J. M. Nouwen (1992)
- ☐ *Hinds' Feet on High Places* by Hannah Hurnard (1955)
- ☐ *The Color of Compromise* by Jemar Tisby (2019)

- ☐ *What's So Amazing about Grace?* by Philip Yancey (1997)
- ☐ *The Ragamuffin Gospel* by Brennan Manning (1990)
- ☐ *Jesus and the Disinherited* by Howard Thurman (1949)
- ☐ *Prophetic Lament* by Soong-Chan Rah (2015)
- ☐ *The Book of Forgiving* by Desmund Tutu and Mpho Tutu (2014)
- ☐ *The Mestizo Augustine* by Justo L. Gonzalez (2016)
- ☐ *One Thousand Gifts* by Ann Voskamp (2011)
- ☐ *Gift from the Sea* by Anne Morrow Lindbergh (1955)
- ☐ *Rescuing the Gospel from the Cowboys* by Richard Twiss (2015)
- ☐ *In a Pit with a Lion on a Snowy Day* by Mark Batterson (2006)
- ☐ *Desiring God* by John Piper (1986)
- ☐ *Orthodoxy* by G. K. Chesterton (1908)
- ☐ *Be the Bridge* by Latasha Morrison (2019)
- ☐ *The Explicit Gospel* by Matt Chandler (2012)
- ☐ *Let Your Life Speak* by Parker Palmer (1999)
- ☐ *The Cost of Discipleship* by Dietrich Bonhoeffer (1937)
- ☐ *Not a Fan* by Kyle Idleman (2011)
- ☐ *Cold-Case Christianity* by J. Warner Wallace (2013)
- ☐ *Celebration of Discipline* by Richard J. Foster (1978)
- ☐ *Liturgy of the Ordinary* by Tish Harrison Warren (2016)
- ☐ *You Are What You Love* by James K. A. Smith (2016)
- ☐ *Captivating* by John and Stasi Eldredge (2005)
- ☐ *The Good and Beautiful God* by James Bryan Smith (2009)
- ☐ *A Year of Biblical Womanhood* by Rachel Held Evans (2012)
- ☐ *Daring Greatly* by Brené Brown (2012)
- ☐ *Love Does* by Bob Goff (2012)
- ☐ *Finding God's Life for My Will* by Mike Donehey (2019)
- ☐ *Unbroken* by Laura Hillenbrand (2010)

FICTION

- ☐ *A Wrinkle in Time* by Madeleine L'Engle (1962)
- ☐ *Gilead* by Marilynne Robinson (2004)
- ☐ *The Pilgrim's Progress* by John Bunyan (1678)
- ☐ *Peace Like a River* by Leif Enger (2002)
- ☐ *In His Steps* by Charles Sheldon (1896)
- ☐ *The Brothers Karamazov* by Fyodor Dostoevsky (1879–1880)
- ☐ *Silence* by Shūsaku Endō (1966)
- ☐ *Redeeming Love* by Francine Rivers (1991)
- ☐ *Christy* by Catherine Marshall (1967)
- ☐ *East of Eden* by John Steinbeck (1952)
- ☐ *The Poisonwood Bible* by Barbara Kingsolver (1998)
- ☐ *The Lord of the Rings* by J.R.R. Tolkien (1954)
- ☐ *Les Misérables* by Victor Hugo (1862)
- ☐ *Their Eyes Were Watching God* by Zora Neale Hurston (1937)
- ☐ *The Robe* by Lloyd C. Douglas (1942)
- ☐ *Ben-Hur* by Lew Wallace (1880)
- ☐ *The Red Tent* by Anita Diamant (1997)
- ☐ *To Kill a Mockingbird* by Harper Lee (1960)
- ☐ *The Lion, the Witch, and the Wardrobe* by C. S. Lewis (1950)
- ☐ *At Home in Mitford* by Jan Karon (1994)
- ☐ *Atonement* by Ian McEwan (2001)
- ☐ *The Violent Bear It Away* by Flannery O'Connor (1960)
- ☐ *Acts of Faith* by Philip Caputo (2005)
- ☐ *The Power and the Glory* by Graham Greene (1940)
- ☐ *A Place on Earth* by Wendell Berry (1966)
- ☐ *The Edge of Sadness* by Edwin O'Connor (1961)
- ☐ *The Last Temptation of Christ* by Nikos Kazantzakis (1952)
- ☐ *My Name Is Asher Lev* by Chaim Potok (1972)

- ☐ *The Screwtape Letters* by C. S. Lewis (1942)
- ☐ *Godric* by Frederick Buechner (1980)
- ☐ *Invisible Man* by Ralph Ellison (1952)
- ☐ *Crossing to Safety* by Wallace Stegner (1987)
- ☐ *Thin Blue Smoke* by Doug Worgul (2009)
- ☐ *Uncle Tom's Cabin* by Harriet Beecher Stowe (1852)
- ☐ *Paradise Lost* by John Milton (1667)
- ☐ *This Present Darkness* by Frank E. Peretti (1986)

MEMOIR

- ☐ *Traveling Mercies* by Anne Lamott (1999)
- ☐ *Just Mercy* by Bryan Stevenson (2014)
- ☐ *Peace Child* by Don Richardson (1974)
- ☐ *Through Gates of Splendor* by Elisabeth Elliot (1957)
- ☐ *A Severe Mercy* by Sheldon Vanauken (1977)
- ☐ *Everything Happens for a Reason* by Kate Bowler (2018)
- ☐ *The Hiding Place* by Corrie ten Boom (1971)
- ☐ *Blue Like Jazz* by Donald Miller (2003)
- ☐ *When Breath Becomes Air* by Paul Kalanithi (2016)
- ☐ *The World as I Remember It* by Rich Mullins (2004)
- ☐ *Night* by Elie Wiesel (1956)
- ☐ *Three Cups of Tea* by Greg Mortenson and David Oliver Relin (2006)
- ☐ *The Unlikely Disciple* by Kevin Roose (2009)
- ☐ *The Cloister Walk* by Kathleen Norris (1996)
- ☐ *Hearts of Fire* by Voice of the Martyrs (2003)
- ☐ *A Prayer Journal* by Flannery O'Connor, edited by W. A. Sessions (2013)

PULITZER PRIZE WINNERS

- ☐ 2025
- ☐ 2024
- ☐ 2023
- ☐ 2022
- ☐ 2021
- ☐ 2020
- ☐ 2019 *The Overstory* by Richard Powers
- ☐ 2018 *Less* by Andrew Sean Greer
- ☐ 2017 *The Underground Railroad* by Colson Whitehead
- ☐ 2016 *The Sympathizer* by Viet Thanh Nguyen
- ☐ 2015 *All the Light We Cannot See* by Anthony Doerr
- ☐ 2014 *The Goldfinch* by Donna Tartt
- ☐ 2013 *The Orphan Master's Son* by Adam Johnson
- ☐ 2012 (No Award)
- ☐ 2011 *A Visit from the Goon Squad* by Jennifer Egan
- ☐ 2010 *Tinkers* by Paul Harding
- ☐ 2009 *Olive Kitteridge* by Elizabeth Strout

- ☐ 2008 *The Brief Wondrous Life of Oscar Wao* by Junot Díaz
- ☐ 2007 *The Road* by Cormac McCarthy
- ☐ 2006 *March* by Geraldine Brooks
- ☐ 2005 *Gilead* by Marilynne Robinson
- ☐ 2004 *The Known World* by Edward P. Jones
- ☐ 2003 *Middlesex* by Jeffrey Eugenides
- ☐ 2002 *Empire Falls* by Richard Russo
- ☐ 2001 *The Amazing Adventures of Kavalier & Clay* by Michael Chabon
- ☐ 2000 *Interpreter of Maladies* by Jhumpa Lahiri
- ☐ 1999 *The Hours* by Michael Cunningham
- ☐ 1998 *American Pastoral* by Philip Roth
- ☐ 1997 *Martin Dressler: The Tale of an American Dreamer* by Steven Millhauser
- ☐ 1996 *Independence Day* by Richard Ford
- ☐ 1995 *The Stone Diaries* by Carol Shields
- ☐ 1994 *The Shipping News* by E. Annie Proulx
- ☐ 1993 *A Good Scent from a Strange Mountain* by Robert Olen Butler
- ☐ 1992 *A Thousand Acres* by Jane Smiley
- ☐ 1991 *Rabbit at Rest* by John Updike
- ☐ 1990 *The Mambo Kings Play Songs of Love* by Oscar Hijuelos
- ☐ 1989 *Breathing Lessons* by Anne Tyler

- ☐ 1988 *Beloved* by Toni Morrison
- ☐ 1987 *A Summons to Memphis* by Peter Taylor
- ☐ 1986 *Lonesome Dove* by Larry McMurtry
- ☐ 1985 *Foreign Affairs* by Alison Lurie
- ☐ 1984 *Ironweed* by William Kennedy
- ☐ 1983 *The Color Purple* by Alice Walker
- ☐ 1982 *Rabbit Is Rich* by John Updike
- ☐ 1981 *A Confederacy of Dunces* by John Kennedy Toole
- ☐ 1980 *The Executioner's Song* by Norman Mailer
- ☐ 1979 *The Stories of John Cheever* by John Cheever
- ☐ 1978 *Elbow Room* by James Alan McPherson
- ☐ 1977 (No Award)
- ☐ 1976 *Humboldt's Gift* by Saul Bellow
- ☐ 1975 *The Killer Angels* by Michael Shaara
- ☐ 1974 (No Award)
- ☐ 1973 *The Optimist's Daughter* by Eudora Welty
- ☐ 1972 *Angle of Repose* by Wallace Stegner
- ☐ 1971 (No Award)
- ☐ 1970 *Collected Stories* by Jean Stafford
- ☐ 1969 *House Made of Dawn* by N. Scott Momaday

- ☐ 1968 *The Confessions of Nat Turner* by William Styron
- ☐ 1967 *The Fixer* by Bernard Malamud
- ☐ 1966 *Collected Stories* by Katherine Anne Porter
- ☐ 1965 *The Keepers of the House* by Shirley Ann Grau
- ☐ 1964 (No Award)
- ☐ 1963 *The Reivers* by William Faulkner
- ☐ 1962 *The Edge of Sadness* by Edwin O'Connor
- ☐ 1961 *To Kill a Mockingbird* by Harper Lee
- ☐ 1960 *Advise and Consent* by Allen Drury
- ☐ 1959 *The Travels of Jaimie McPheeters* by Robert Lewis Taylor
- ☐ 1958 *A Death in the Family* by James Agee
- ☐ 1957 (No Award)
- ☐ 1956 *Andersonville* by MacKinlay Kantor
- ☐ 1955 *A Fable* by William Faulkner
- ☐ 1954 (No Award)
- ☐ 1953 *The Old Man and the Sea* by Ernest Hemingway
- ☐ 1952 *The Caine Mutiny* by Herman Wouk
- ☐ 1951 *The Town* by Conrad Richter
- ☐ 1950 *The Way West* by A. B. Guthrie Jr.
- ☐ 1949 *Guard of Honor* by James Gould Cozzens
- ☐ 1948 *Tales of the South Pacific* by James A. Michener

BBC: TOP 100 READS

- ☐ *The Lord of the Rings* by J. R. R. Tolkien
- ☐ *Pride and Prejudice* by Jane Austen
- ☐ *His Dark Materials* by Philip Pullman
- ☐ *The Hitchhiker's Guide to the Galaxy* by Douglas Adams
- ☐ *Harry Potter and the Goblet of Fire* by J. K. Rowling
- ☐ *To Kill a Mockingbird* by Harper Lee
- ☐ *Winnie-the-Pooh* by A. A. Milne
- ☐ *1984* by George Orwell
- ☐ *The Lion, the Witch, and the Wardrobe* by C. S. Lewis
- ☐ *Jane Eyre* by Charlotte Brontë
- ☐ *Catch-22* by Joseph Heller
- ☐ *Wuthering Heights* by Emily Brontë
- ☐ *Birdsong* by Sebastian Faulks
- ☐ *Rebecca* by Daphne du Maurier
- ☐ *The Catcher in the Rye* by J. D. Salinger
- ☐ *The Wind in the Willows* by Kenneth Grahame
- ☐ *Great Expectations* by Charles Dickens
- ☐ *Little Women* by Louisa May Alcott
- ☐ *Captain Corelli's Mandolin* by Louis de Bernières
- ☐ *War and Peace* by Leo Tolstoy
- ☐ *Gone with the Wind* by Margaret Mitchell
- ☐ *Harry Potter and the Philosopher's Stone* by J. K. Rowling
- ☐ *Harry Potter and the Chamber of Secrets* by J. K. Rowling
- ☐ *Harry Potter and the Prisoner of Azkaban* by J. K. Rowling
- ☐ *The Hobbit* by J. R. R. Tolkien
- ☐ *Tess of the d'Urbervilles* by Thomas Hardy
- ☐ *Middlemarch* by George Eliot

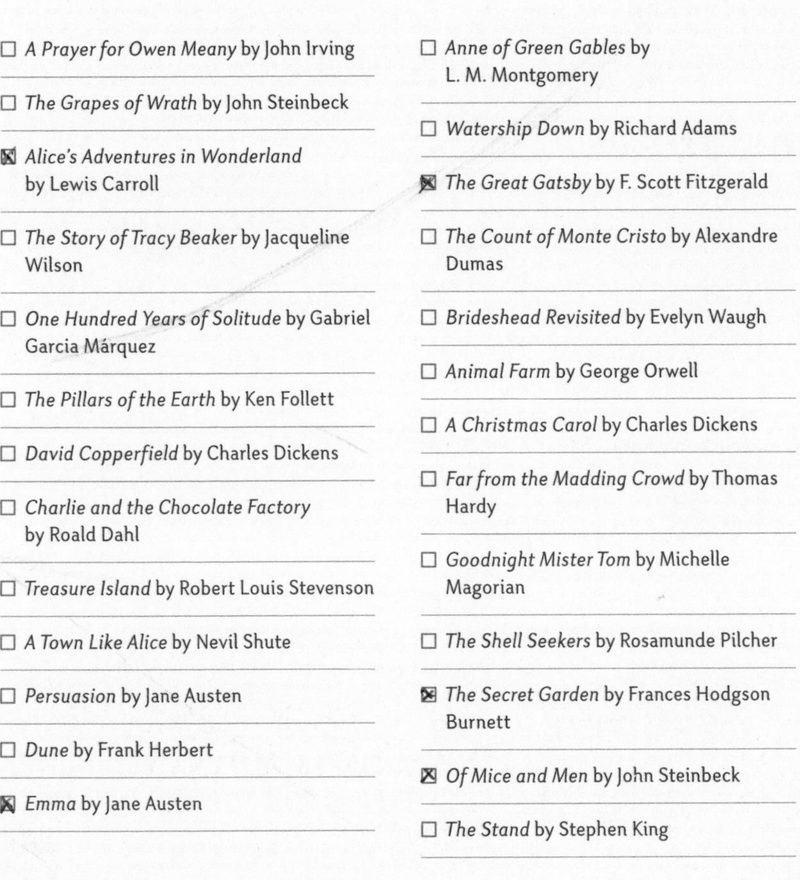

- [ ] *A Prayer for Owen Meany* by John Irving
- [ ] *The Grapes of Wrath* by John Steinbeck
- [x] *Alice's Adventures in Wonderland* by Lewis Carroll
- [ ] *The Story of Tracy Beaker* by Jacqueline Wilson
- [ ] *One Hundred Years of Solitude* by Gabriel Garcia Márquez
- [ ] *The Pillars of the Earth* by Ken Follett
- [ ] *David Copperfield* by Charles Dickens
- [ ] *Charlie and the Chocolate Factory* by Roald Dahl
- [ ] *Treasure Island* by Robert Louis Stevenson
- [ ] *A Town Like Alice* by Nevil Shute
- [ ] *Persuasion* by Jane Austen
- [ ] *Dune* by Frank Herbert
- [x] *Emma* by Jane Austen
- [ ] *Anne of Green Gables* by L. M. Montgomery
- [ ] *Watership Down* by Richard Adams
- [x] *The Great Gatsby* by F. Scott Fitzgerald
- [ ] *The Count of Monte Cristo* by Alexandre Dumas
- [ ] *Brideshead Revisited* by Evelyn Waugh
- [ ] *Animal Farm* by George Orwell
- [ ] *A Christmas Carol* by Charles Dickens
- [ ] *Far from the Madding Crowd* by Thomas Hardy
- [ ] *Goodnight Mister Tom* by Michelle Magorian
- [ ] *The Shell Seekers* by Rosamunde Pilcher
- [x] *The Secret Garden* by Frances Hodgson Burnett
- [x] *Of Mice and Men* by John Steinbeck
- [ ] *The Stand* by Stephen King

- ☐ *Anna Karenina* by Leo Tolstoy
- ☐ *A Suitable Boy* by Vikram Seth
- ☐ *The BFG* by Roald Dahl
- ☐ *Swallows and Amazons* by Arthur Ransome
- ☐ *Black Beauty* by Anna Sewell
- ☐ *Artemis Fowl* by Eoin Colfer
- ☐ *Crime and Punishment* by Fyodor Dostoevsky
- ☐ *Noughts and Crosses* by Malorie Blackman
- ☐ *Memoirs of a Geisha* by Arthur Golden
- ☐ *A Tale of Two Cities* by Charles Dickens
- ☐ *The Thorn Birds* by Colleen McCullough
- ☐ *Mort* by Terry Pratchett
- ☐ *The Magic Faraway Tree* by Enid Blyton
- ☐ *The Magus* by John Fowles
- ☐ *Good Omens* by Terry Pratchett and Neil Gaiman
- ☐ *Guards! Guards!* by Terry Pratchett
- ☐ *Lord of the Flies* by William Golding
- ☐ *Perfume* by Patrick Süskind
- ☐ *The Ragged Trousered Philanthropists* by Robert Tressell
- ☐ *Night Watch* by Terry Pratchett
- ☐ *Matilda* by Roald Dahl
- ☐ *Bridget Jones's Diary* by Helen Fielding
- ☐ *The Secret History* by Donna Tartt
- ☐ *The Woman in White* by Wilkie Collins
- ☐ *Ulysses* by James Joyce
- ☐ *Bleak House* by Charles Dickens
- ☐ *Double Act* by Jacqueline Wilson
- ☐ *The Twits* by Roald Dahl
- ☐ *I Capture the Castle* by Dodie Smith
- ☐ *Holes* by Louis Sachar
- ☐ *Gormenghast* by Mervyn Peake
- ☐ *The God of Small Things* by Arundhati Roy

- ☐ *Vicky Angel* by Jacqueline Wilson
- ☐ *Brave New World* by Aldous Huxley
- ☐ *Cold Comfort Farm* by Stella Gibbons
- ☐ *Magician* by Raymond E. Feist
- ☐ *On the Road* by Jack Kerouac
- ☐ *The Godfather* by Mario Puzo
- ☐ *The Clan of the Cave Bear* by Jean M. Auel
- ☐ *The Colour of Magic* by Terry Pratchett
- ☐ *The Alchemist* by Paulo Coelho
- ☐ *Katherine* by Anya Seton
- ☐ *Kane and Abel* by Jeffrey Archer
- ☐ *Love in the Time of Cholera* by Gabriel García Márquez
- ☐ *Girls in Love* by Jacqueline Wilson
- ☐ *The Princess Diaries* by Meg Cabot
- ☐ *Midnight's Children* by Salman Rushdie

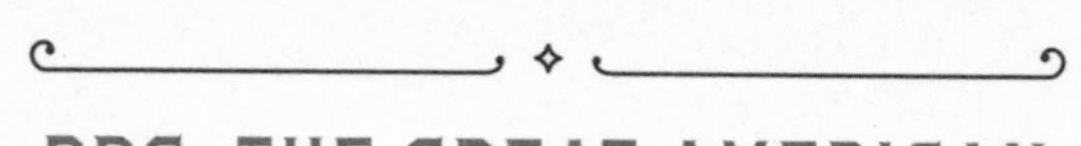

PBS: THE GREAT AMERICAN READ

- ☐ *To Kill a Mockingbird* by Harper Lee
- ☐ *Outlander* (series) by Diana Gabaldon
- ☐ *Harry Potter* (series) by J. K. Rowling
- ☐ *Pride and Prejudice* by Jane Austen
- ☐ *The Lord of the Rings* (series) by J. R. R. Tolkien
- ☐ *Gone with the Wind* by Margaret Mitchell
- ☐ *Charlotte's Web* by E. B. White
- ☐ *Little Women* by Louisa May Alcott
- ☐ *The Chronicles of Narnia* (series) by C. S. Lewis
- ☐ *Jane Eyre* by Charlotte Brontë
- ☐ *Anne of Green Gables* by L. M. Montgomery
- ☐ *The Grapes of Wrath* by John Steinbeck
- ☐ *A Tree Grows in Brooklyn* by Betty Smith
- ☐ *The Book Thief* by Marcus Zusak
- ☐ *The Great Gatsby* by F. Scott Fitzgerald
- ☐ *The Help* by Kathryn Stockett
- ☐ *The Adventures of Tom Sawyer* by Mark Twain
- ☐ *1984* by George Orwell
- ☐ *And Then There Were None* by Agatha Christie
- ☐ *Atlas Shrugged* by Ayn Rand
- ☐ *Wuthering Heights* by Emily Brontë
- ☐ *Lonesome Dove* by Larry McMurtry
- ☐ *The Pillars of the Earth* by Ken Follett
- ☐ *The Stand* by Stephen King
- ☐ *Rebecca* by Daphne du Maurier
- ☐ *A Prayer for Owen Meany* by John Irving
- ☐ *The Color Purple* by Alice Walker
- ☐ *Alice's Adventures in Wonderland* by Lewis Carroll

- ☐ *Great Expectations* by Charles Dickens
- ☐ *The Catcher in the Rye* by J. D. Salinger
- ☐ *Where the Red Fern Grows* by Wilson Rawls
- ☐ *The Outsiders* by S. E. Hinton
- ☐ *The Da Vinci Code* by Dan Brown
- ☐ *The Handmaid's Tale* by Margaret Atwood
- ☐ *Dune* by Frank Herbert
- ☐ *The Little Prince* by Antoine de Saint-Exupéry
- ☐ *The Call of the Wild* by Jack London
- ☐ *The Clan of the Cave Bear* by Jean M. Auel
- ☐ *The Hitchhiker's Guide to the Galaxy* by Douglas Adams
- ☐ *The Hunger Games* (series) by Suzanne Collins
- ☐ *The Count of Monte Cristo* by Alexandre Dumas
- ☐ *The Joy Luck Club* by Amy Tan
- ☐ *Frankenstein* by Mary Shelley
- ☐ *The Giver* by Lois Lowry
- ☐ *Memoirs of a Geisha* by Arthur Golden
- ☐ *Moby Dick* by Herman Melville
- ☐ *Catch-22* by Joseph Heller
- ☐ *Game of Thrones* (series) by George R. R. Martin
- ☐ *Foundation* (series) by Isaac Asimov
- ☐ *War and Peace* by Leo Tolstoy
- ☐ *Their Eyes Were Watching God* by Zora Neale Hurston
- ☐ *Jurassic Park* by Michael Crichton
- ☐ *The Godfather* by Mario Puzo
- ☐ *One Hundred Years of Solitude* by Gabriel García Márquez
- ☐ *The Picture of Dorian Gray* by Oscar Wilde
- ☐ *The Notebook* by Nicholas Sparks
- ☐ *The Shack* by William Paul Young
- ☐ *A Confederacy of Dunces* by John Kennedy Toole
- ☐ *The Hunt for Red October* by Tom Clancy
- ☐ *Beloved* by Toni Morrison

- ☐ *The Martian* by Andy Weir
- ☐ *The Wheel of Time* (series) by Robert Jordan
- ☐ *Siddhartha* by Hermann Hesse
- ☐ *Crime and Punishment* by Fyodor Dostoevsky
- ☐ *The Sun Also Rises* by Ernest Hemingway
- ☐ *The Curious Incident of the Dog in the Night-time* by Mark Haddon
- ☐ *A Separate Peace* by John Knowles
- ☐ *Don Quixote* by Miguel de Cervantes
- ☐ *The Lovely Bones* by Alice Sebold
- ☐ *The Alchemist* by Paulo Coelho
- ☐ *Hatchet* (series) by Gary Paulsen
- ☐ *Invisible Man* by Ralph Ellison
- ☐ *The Twilight Saga* (series) by Stephanie Meyer
- ☐ *Tales of the City* (series) by Armistead Maupin
- ☐ *Gulliver's Travels* by Jonathan Swift
- ☐ *Ready Player One* by Ernest Cline
- ☐ *Left Behind* (series) by Tim LaHaye and Jerry B. Jenkins
- ☐ *Gone Girl* by Gillian Flynn
- ☐ *Watchers* by Dean Koontz
- ☐ *The Pilgrim's Progress* by John Bunyan
- ☐ Alex Cross Mysteries (series) by James Patterson
- ☐ *Things Fall Apart* by Chinua Achebe
- ☐ *Heart of Darkness* by Joseph Conrad
- ☐ *Gilead* by Marilynne Robinson
- ☐ *Flowers in the Attic* by V. C. Andrews
- ☐ *Fifty Shades of Grey* (series) by E. L. James
- ☐ *The Sirens of Titan* by Kurt Vonnegut
- ☐ *This Present Darkness* by Frank E. Peretti
- ☐ *Americanah* by Chimamanda Ngozi Adichie

- ☐ *Another Country* by James Baldwin
- ☐ *Bless Me, Ultima* by Rudolfo Anaya
- ☐ *Looking for Alaska* by John Green
- ☐ *The Brief Wondrous Life of Oscar Wao* by Junot Díaz
- ☐ *Swan Song* by Robert R. McCammon
- ☐ *Mind Invaders* by Dave Hunt
- ☐ *White Teeth* by Zadie Smith
- ☐ *Ghost* by Jason Reynolds
- ☐ *The Coldest Winter Ever* by Sister Souljah
- ☐ *The Intuitionist* by Colson Whitehead
- ☐ *Doña Bárbara* by Rómulo Gallegos

JUSTO L. GONZÁLEZ

BIRTH	POPULAR WORKS	AWARDS
August 9, 1937 *Havana, Cuba* GENRE *Theology and Church History*	A History of Christian Thought; The Story of Christianity, Vol. 1; The Story of Christianity, Vol. 2	*Ecumenism Award from Washington Theological Consortium, numerous Honorary Doctorates*

Born and raised in Cuba, Dr. Justo L. González has written more than one hundred books on the history of Christianity, theology, and the Latino experience in the United States. He attended seminary in Cuba and earned his PhD in historical theology from Yale. A retired professor of theology, González continues to contribute to the study, focusing on and promoting programs for the theological education of Hispanics.

Both of his most popular works have been translated and are commonly used as textbooks for seminaries and universities, yet are very readable and accessible. As González himself wrote in *A History of Christian Thought*, they "serve as an introduction to the subject for readers with little or no theological training, giving them both the basic knowledge needed for further theological and historical studies and a vision of the rich variety of Christian thought through the ages."

In his introduction to *The Story of Christianity, Vol. 1*, González writes, "As we look at those and other past times and events, we do so through the lens of our own time, our own concerns, our own hopes. History is not the pure past; history is a past interpreted from the present of the historian." Since Latinos make up nearly 20 percent of the US population and are one of the driving forces in the ongoing vitality of Christianity around the world, it's more critical than ever to expand our awareness of their cultural contribution. Dr. Justo González's work continues to equip and teach Christians around the world.

BOOKS I WANT TO READ

Use these next few pages to create your own TBR (to be read) list. Refer to the book lists on pages 186–201 for ideas and inspiration.

ANSWER KEY TO "WHO WROTE IT?" (PAGE 152)

1—C, Leo Tolstoy, *Anna Karenina*

2—N, Oscar Wilde, *The Picture of Dorian Gray*

3—B, Harper Lee, *To Kill a Mockingbird*

4—O, William Shakespeare, *Hamlet*

5—A, John Green, *The Fault in Our Stars*

6—L, Jane Austen, *Pride and Prejudice*

7—F, Dr. Seuss, *Oh, The Places You'll Go!*

8—J, Maya Angelou, *I Know Why the Caged Bird Sings*

9—E, Antoine de Saint-Exupéry, *The Little Prince*

10—I, Stephen King, *Rita Hayworth and the Shawshank Redemption*

11—H, J.R.R. Tolkien, *The Lord of the Rings*

12—G, Toni Morrison, *Beloved*

13—K, Charles Dickens, *A Tale of Two Cities*

14—M, F. Scott Fitzgerald, *The Great Gatsby*

15—D, George Orwell, *1984*

NOTES

Page 41. Written using the following sources: Karen Wright Marsh, "The Demanding Faith of Flannery O'Connor," *Christianity Today,* September 13, 2017, www.christianitytoday.com/women/2017/september/demanding-faith-flannery-oconnor.html; A Prayer Journal by Flannery O'Conner, edited by W. A. Sessions (Farrar, Straus, and Giroux, 2013); and Colleen Carroll Campbell, "Flannery O'Connor Instructs Catholics to 'Stalk Joy in Scandal Time,'" Religion New Service, March 26, 2019, https://religionnews.com/2019/03/26/flannery-oconnor-instructs-catholics-to-stalk-joy-in-scandal-time/.

Page 77. Written using the following sources: https://en.wikipedia.org/wiki/Sh%C5%ABsaku_End%C5%8D; https://us.macmillan.com/books/9781250082275; Shūsaku Endō, Silence (Picador Books, 1969).

Page 113. Written using the following sources: Frederick Douglass, *Narrative of the Life of Frederick Douglass, an American Slave* (First Signet Class Printing, 1997); Frederick Douglass, *My Bondage and My Freedom* (Dover Publications, 1969); and Philip S. Foner and Yuval Taylor (editors), *Frederick Douglass: Selected Speeches and Writings* (Chicago Review Books, 1999).

Page 149. Written using the following sources: "About Dorothy L. Sayers," The Dorothy L. Sayers Society, www.sayers.org.uk/biography; "Dorothy Sayers,"

The Guardian, July 22, 2008, www.theguardian.com/books/2008/jun/11/dorothylsayers; and Crystal Downing, "Dorothy Sayers Did Not Want to Be a Prophet," *Christianity Today*, May 18, 2018, www.christianitytoday.com/ct/2018/june/dorothy-sayers-reluctant-prophet.html.

Page 185. Written using the following sources: Cornelia Seigneur, "A Native Faith: Richard Twiss Shapes Portland's Youth and Beyond," *Christianity Today*, February 16, 2012, www.christianitytoday.com/thisisourcity/portland/anativefaith.html?paging=off; Gordon Govier, "Remembering Richard Twiss," InterVarsity Press, February 14, 2013, intervarsity.org/news/remembering-richard-twiss; and en.wikipedia.org/wiki/Richard_Twiss.

Page 203. Written using the following sources: Justo L. González, Author, HarperCollins Publishers, www.harpercollins.com/author/cr-106158/justo-l-gonzalez/; Justo L. González, Author, InterVarsity Press, www.ivpress.com/justo-l-gonzalez; Justo L. González, *The Story of Christianity, Vol. 1: The Early Church to the Dawn of the Reformation* (HarperOne, 2010), 5; and Justo L. González, *A History of Christian Thought, Vol. 1: From the Beginnings to the Council of Chalcedon* (Abingdon Press, 1987).

Book trivia factoids were taken from the following sources: *Remarkable Books: The World's Most Beautiful and Historic Works* (DK, 2017); hellogiggles.com; www.barnesandnoble.com/blog; www.englishclub.com; blog.anypromo.com/36-fun-facts-books/; www.guinnessworldrecords.com/news/2018/10/5-page-turning-book-facts; bookstr.com/list/14-facts-about-books-and-reading-for-the-fanatical-bookworm/; www.stylist.co.uk/books/everyday-sayings-explained/124076; www.sturgislibrary.org/history/oldest-library/; www.abebooks.com/blog/2009/02/12/25-random-things-about-reading; www.maryjowegnerarboretum.com/news_publications/newsroom.html/article/2018/10/08/how-reading-makes-you-a-better-person; electricliterature.com/9-mind-blowing-facts-about-your-favorite-books/; and allthatsinteresting.com/six-surprising-author-facts.